Pengu

WicKeD BuT ViRTuoUS

Mirka Mora was born in Paris in 1928 and moved to Melbourne
in 1951, where she soon made a name for herself in what was
then a very male-dominated art world. She uses a wide range
of media and her work features strongly in the permanent
collection of Melbourne's Museum of Modern Art at
Heide. For many years she has conducted workshops
in painting, soft sculpture and mosaics, where
countless Australians have learned from her
unique approach to teaching art. In 2002
Mirka Mora was made an *Officier de
l'Ordre des Arts et des Lettres* by the
French Minister of Culture
and Communication. She
lives in a studio in
Richmond.

to Dear Helen
with love
Suwanir
25/12/09.

WiCKeD BUT ViRTuouS

MY LiFe MiRKa MoRa

PENGUIN BOOKS

PENGUIN BOOKS

Published by the Penguin Group
Penguin Group (Australia)
250 Camberwell Road, Camberwell, Victoria 3124, Australia
(a division of Pearson Australia Group Pty Ltd)
Penguin Group (USA) Inc.
375 Hudson Street, New York, New York 10014, USA
Penguin Group (Canada)
90 Eglinton Avenue East, Suite 700, Toronto, Canada ON M4P 2Y3
(a division of Pearson Penguin Canada Inc.)
Penguin Books Ltd
80 Strand, London WC2R 0RL England
Penguin Ireland
25 St Stephen's Green, Dublin 2, Ireland
(a division of Penguin Books Ltd)
Penguin Books India Pvt Ltd
11 Community Centre, Panchsheel Park, New Delhi – 110 017, India
Penguin Group (NZ)
67 Apollo Drive, Rosedale, North Shore 0632, New Zealand
(a division of Pearson New Zealand Ltd)
Penguin Books (South Africa) (Pty) Ltd
24 Sturdee Avenue, Rosebank, Johannesburg 2196, South Africa

Penguin Books Ltd, Registered Offices: 80 Strand, London, WC2R 0RL, England

First published by Penguin Books Australia 2000
First published in paperback 2002

10 9 8 7 6 5 4 3

Copyright © in the text and text illustrations Mirka Mora 2000
Paintings copyright © Mirka Mora. All paintings appear
courtesy of William Mora Galleries and the artist.
For copyright in photographs, see Photograph Sources

The moral right of the author has been asserted

All rights reserved. Without limiting the rights under copyright reserved above, no part of this publication
may be reproduced, stored in or introduced into a retrieval system, or transmitted, in any form or by any
means (electronic, mechanical, photocopying, recording or otherwise), without the prior written permission
of both the copyright owner and the above publisher of this book.

Cover design by Melissa Fraser, Penguin Design Studio
Front cover painting, *When the Soul Sleeps*, 1970; and back cover painting, detail from *Mother and Child on Bird*, 1970, by Mirka Mora
Text design by Sandy Cull
Typeset in Granjon by Post Pre-press Group, Brisbane, Queensland
Printed and bound in Australia by McPherson's Printing Group, Maryborough, Victoria

National Library of Australia
Cataloguing-in-Publication data:

Mora, Mirka, 1928– .
  Wicked but virtuous: my life.

  Bibliography.
  Includes index.
  ISBN 978 0 14 029483 5

  1. Mora, Mirka, 1928– . 2. Artists – Australia – Biography. 3 Women artists – Australia – Biography.
  4. Painting, Modern – 20th century – Australia. I. Title.

759.994

This project has been assisted by the Commonwealth Government through the Australia Council, its arts
funding and advisory body.

Australia | Council
for the Arts

penguin.com.au

To all my cats, to all my family,
and to all the men I've loved

Nul homme
ne peut dire ce qu'il est, mais il arrive
qu'il ait conclu . . . le soleil n'outrepassera
pas ses bornes. Sinon les Erinnyes qui gardent
la justice sauront le découvrir.

No man can say what he is, but it happens that he
has concluded . . . the sun will not overpass its
boundary. If it does, the ancient Greek goddesses
who are guarding Justice will know how to
find him out.

ALBERT CAMUS
(translation: Mirka Mora)

CONTENTS

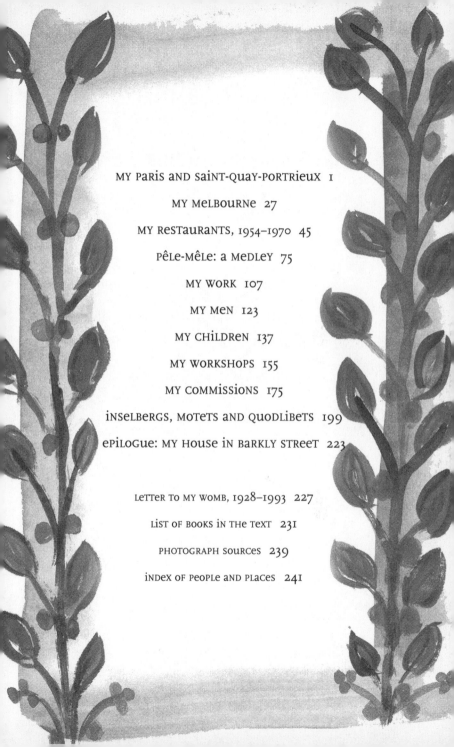

MY PARIS AND SAINT-QUAY-PORTRIEUX

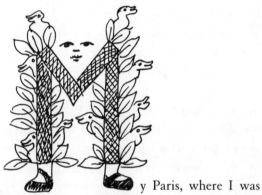

y Paris, where I was born on 18th March 1928, on a Sunday afternoon at 3pm. My mother had waited for me for a month in the Hospital Rothschild, helping wherever she could, but after a month went back home and then I decided to enter the world. There was a lovely nurse whose name, Madeleine, my parents gave me as well as Mirka, which was the name of my maternal Romanian grandmother.

My maternal grandfather was a blacksmith and painter who decorated lovely carts and buggies. My paternal grandfather was a printer, a typographer as they were called in those days. He was famous for losing his temper on an operating table, circa 1910. He got up and went home with his tummy open and lived to tell the tale. My paternal grandparents had twelve daughters, all very beautiful, and the thirteenth child was a boy, my father. Grandma looked very old by the age of forty, from photographs I saw in 1938.

One my father had from his mother and one was sent to my mother from her mother, very poignant and brave. I was hypnotised by her handwriting as my mother read the text written on the back of the postcard to her three little girls.

During the First World War there was terrible persecution against Jewish people in Lithuania, where my father lived, and in Romania where my mother was born and lived. My father, who was born in 1899, was sixteen when he was told by good people in the forest on his way home to run for his life, for Jewish boys were being killed. My poor dad never saw his parents again, and walked his way through Germany where he ate snakes and monkeys in tins and eventually found his way to Paris.

He was very handsome and his first job was to be a model in the sculpture school at the Louvre. *Incroyable mais vrai!* (Unbelievable but true!) My father told me this as I said goodbye to him when I left Paris for Melbourne. He also told me that if I became famous I must not forget that I'd come from very humble people, which was very intriguing.

My mother, in Romania, after having her little shop ransacked – she had bags of walnuts and potatoes for sale, and a little sewing machine – decided to leave her lovely parents and with her brother settled to go to New York. They had to reach Rotterdam first and wait three years for a boat, circa 1920. When the boat arrived, their tickets were stolen and they aimed for Paris; there my mother met my father. My uncle did go to New York on a new ticket.

In Paris it was the Depression, but my father seemed to fend for himself and this was one of the reasons my mother married him, so I was told. Three daughters were born: Marcelle, the youngest; Salomèe (who always wrote her name like that, with *un accent grave*), the middle one; and myself, Mirka Madeleine, the oldest. When I was four years old, a beautiful woman who lived across the street and who waved to me fell in love with me. It was 214 rue de Crimée. My mother, who was *une mère poule*, very possessive of her daughter, still agreed to lend me to the lady, Paulette, every weekend and during school holidays. It was remarkable that my mother could see how Paulette would enhance my education. During weekends I would listen again and again to Jules Massenet's *amoureuses* – sacred and profane arias. They marked me for life.

My double life started. Paulette's stepmother, Nouzette, with whom Paulette would leave me sometimes when she had to go away for work, was a strong Catholic. Nouzette would go to church early in the morning, then in the afternoon, *vespéral*.

It was very puzzling for me as she would leave me alone in her beautiful country house in Saint-James, near Fougères, in lower Normandie. I dream to go back to 14 rue de Fougères. I would wait for her, hiding under the round table in the middle of the room downstairs. At Christmas she would take me to church to show me the nativity scene, which entranced me. The incense burner swinging, held by a priest dressed in white, made me dizzy, awakening all my senses. At home she would teach me to count: division and multiplication, addition and subtraction. I would get some money when I was right, twenty-five centimes, ten sous.

She would teach me all the prayers secretly, and all was well every summertime until one summer when I went to the toilet at the bottom of the garden. I stayed in there a very, very long time. The cause of my being so long away was a large spider on the wall and I could not do it, the poop. The spider was very furry, glued to the middle of the white wall, at my eye level, staring at me and I at it, a bit of light on its black shimmering fur from the open door.

The spider was at the same spot every day right through the summer. As the dunny was too far from the house, if I called I would not have been heard. Anyhow, I was so petrified that I could not call, thinking the sound of my words would make it jump onto me; I also feared to move and all my good intentions of emptying my bowels disappeared. I could not pooh any more. My long absence was noticed and I was rescued and then punished when I told Nouzette that I was praying to the Virgin Mary, asking her to tell the spider to go away and make me do *caca*.

At age seven or eight I thought one could pray anywhere when you needed help, especially to the Virgin Mary, who winked at me in the church every time I went there. I thought the punishment was a little severe and it made me cry. The punishment was to kneel on Nouzette's big bed underneath the print of the thorned Christ with blood dripping on his forehead. He was praying also, I thought. I had to ask forgiveness, it took a long time.

I became constipated right throughout the summer, and when Paulette finally returned, a new regime started with my problem. Every night the two ladies sharpened a piece of savon de Marseille in the shape of a pointy bullet and introduced it into my anus for the night. The idea was that it would cure my constipation regardless of the visiting spider, on whom the ray of sun landed when it came to sunbake everyday. When the bullets didn't work I was given charcoal to chew and swallow. No wonder I did so many charcoal drawings later, passionately.

Otherwise, the three of us had lovely holidays in the south of France – Port-Cros, Bandol, Nice, Cannes – or north-west in Dinard, Deauville, Saint-Malo, Le Mont-Saint-Michel, Honfleur, and many other lovely parts of France.

But it was Saint-James that I loved the most as a child, the forests surrounding the village full of big mushrooms – *cèpes* – lily of the valley; and *mâche*, a tasty salad to pick in the fields, a little nutty in taste and served with cooked beetroot. The little river where a man made clogs with the wood from the forest. The sound of the river where the water ran fast, the smell of freshly cut wood. The cemetery where Nouzette's husband was buried, his grave covered with myosotis, little blue flowers, a humble tomb. We went there often to trim the flowers; Nouzette was a great expert at weeding and taught me how to do it. Weeding in the vegetable garden took a lot of our time, also tying up the mignonettes so their hearts would be white and not green. Catching the snails was my job and they always escaped because I didn't put a heavy stone on the lid. I was proud of the snails escaping. Across the street there were three large, elderly ladies who dressed in black and gave me dragées when we went to visit them for afternoon tea. From one of their windows I could see into the forest, where I thought wolves lived.

I loved listening to tales of events in Saint-James. One was about a woman who had been found dead on her back on the floor of her kitchen, with a long snake that went through her vagina and came out of her mouth. Another tale was about a little child in his cot playing with a hammer, and as his grandmother passed by, the child hit the grandmother with the hammer and she died. Stories you never forget, and love.

My time with Nouzette was spent singing, dancing, and going for long walks as we collected hazelnuts along the road, eating bread and butter tartines covered with chives. We visited hospitals where once I tried, on my tiptoes, to look inside the little bed to see the baby, but instead there was a dwarf. Big surprise, no explanations.

At night I slept with Nouzette in her very big and high

wooden bed, below the large print of the Virgin Mary and the one of Christ with a crown of thorns over his forehead. My big game was to be followed by their eyes as I moved around the room, when I was again left alone and not under the table. I loved that room with its two windows overlooking the street. The grandfather clock, the big bed, the big *cuisinière* with its hot-water tap, a big trunk on which I stood after my bath to be dried with a warm towel. The round table in the middle of the room, a *colimaçon* stairway going upstairs and the door always open, going to the garden outside. The cellar, the aviary, the library. In the little court separating the house from the garden we often played, Paulette, Nouzette and I, bouncing my big ball.

Hanging on the stairway wall were sabres, swords and guns, not unlike the ones my father collected from the Franco–Prussian war in the 1870s. When Paulette came I would sleep with her, upstairs in these provincial bedrooms wallpapered with unforgettable designs. Hanging on the wall was a Raphael print of the Mother and Child and the pink wallpaper was a Jouy design, eighteenth-century France, *scènes champêtres à la Watteau*. The scent of lavender was in every room. There was a giant seashell from New Caledonia where Paulette's brother, an officer, was stationed. He had a wife who always used the bidet after each visit to the toilet, and it was cause for great wonder and long conversations.

There was also my favourite place beside the cellar, which smelt of fresh cream and apples, and the vegetable garden with bees. The library where I was left alone often and in ecstasy. The smell of old books. Paulette's father had been killed in the First World War and his presence in the library was very potent: all the pencils well sharpened and left there as they always had been on the bureau, pointy ends facing up. It was in his library that I discovered

Les Images d'epinal. Stories with pictures coloured in red, blue and yellow with black outlines, and also bookshelves from top to bottom on each wall, enveloping me.

In *Les Images d'epinal*, my favourite story, which always made me cry, was *'Le Lion reconnaissant et Androclès'*, the story about a slave who ran away to the desert and met a lion with a sore and bloodied paw. Androcles takes out the thorn and the lion goes to sleep and puts his paw on Androcles' leg. Three years pass and Androcles goes away and gets caught and taken to the arena to be eaten by the lions. But one lion comes close to the slave and licks his hand, recognising his friend from the desert. The emperor was stunned and accorded freedom to Androcles, and in town the lion was often seen walking with Androcles, the lion held by a little strap.

One picture that I remember especially was of a little child holding an umbrella and flying in the sky over a village. There was another picture of two men, one thin and one fat, run over by a steamroller; the thin one got very long and the fat one got very large and flat on the road. I thought it was sheer wonder and marvelled at it every time I opened the book on that very page. The book had also lots of angels with long robes flying over little villages – again, high in the sky. It was a very, very large book full of engraved pictures.

Below the library was the aviary full of pigeons; I could hear them cooing. Nouzette would get one or two for dinner and I used to watch her putting the pigeon's head in a basin full of water and waiting until the bird's wings would stop flapping. I could never eat meat as a child and always made sure Mistigris the cat would be under my chair so that I could pass the meat to Mistigris, and for a reward I would take Mistigris on my knees, sitting on a chair near the grandfather clock for hours, as I loved listening to the *tic-toc* it made in the quiet house. It was also fun to watch through the windows into the street when a horse and cart passed. With any luck the horse would leave a present – the ladies, with a shovel, picking up the horse's manure for their garden. They were fast, like blackbirds as they all wore black, probably all First World War widows like Nouzette was. Nouzette was the prettiest, very slim with her grey plaits around her head and green eyes, smiling eyes.

In the south of France I had been very scared of the mistral, which is a fierce wind. I also had been punished by Paulette because I held my tummy with my arm as I was photographed, aged nine perhaps, but the perfumed wattle and the crickets were enchanting and I found them all waiting for me in Australia, thirteen years later.

Back in Paris, and to school, after the holidays and my different sets of clothes and shoes and food and tempo and atmosphere – a family. I loved school passionately. When I could not find a word or an arithmetic solution, I would stare intently at the blackboard, thinking it would print the answer for me. After school I wondered where the teachers went, as I didn't think they were normal human beings like the rest of us. One day in springtime, when I was twelve, my mother was a little late to pick me up. When I saw my lady teacher leaving school and meeting and kissing a man, I realised that teachers were human beings and I understood something, but I didn't know what it was.

On the way to school, boys would throw stones at us, so if I saw them coming I would take my two little sisters and cross the street to avoid them. I didn't like the noisy playground and rough girls pushing and shoving. I only loved being in the classroom and learning all the different subjects. Every month, if you were a good student, you received the *croix d'honneur* or the *croix d'excellence*.

I always won the *croix d'honneur* and wore it attached to a beautiful ribbon on my dress or *tablier noir*. I usually sat at a desk in front of the teacher with a girl sitting next to me. One time, when it was grape season, the girl taught me how to squash a grape into my vagina through my underpants, right under the teacher's nose. It went on for days and the teacher never caught us.

At home, sometimes we were poor, living in a one-room apartment; sometimes things got better and we lived in a large apartment. The rue de Crimée apartment was very large. After the au pair girl disappeared with my mother's clothes and left debts in each shop in the street, we were left alone many a time and it was my job to look after my sisters. I warmed up the baby bottle for my sister Marcelle, standing on a chair at the stove. I didn't like glass on paintings and drawings and I constantly broke the glass on the clocks and photographs. One hot summer I turned the flat into a swimming pool for my sisters, opening all the taps in the flat. When my mother came home I had to go with her to apologise to the lady who lived below our flat. The water had gone right through to her bedroom and onto her bed and little cushions. The lady was very kind to my mother and I never forgot her kindness, even though I was so young.

When my sisters got a bit bigger they often locked me out on the window sill and people would assemble below, waiting for me to fall off. Once, when I was locked out on the window sill, I saw my mother running home just as Marcelle, who had escaped the flat, missed being hit by a car. My mother saw my sister and then me on the window sill at the same time. Another time, I managed to throw my parents' large mattress out of the window of the third floor where we lived, with the help of my little sisters. A great feat which psychiatrists would love. When my sisters got a bit bigger still, they often locked me into cupboards. I was a fool, always getting in where it was dark and cosy, like a cat, being rescued when our parents came home.

The flat I lived in from the age of twelve until the war and after was 7 rue Maître Albert, with a view of Notre-Dame and the River Seine. My father took me to see the previous owner still in his flat, whose walls were covered with paintings in every room. At a certain time, the two men went into another room and left me near a *premier Empire* buffet, with a sculpture level to my nose. As I lifted my face to investigate the little sculpture I saw it was a nymph, naked, lying on her back, with a beautiful satyr bending over the nymph. Somehow I understood something, but what was it? I didn't know. I knew about horses' penises but that satyr's was an unusual pointy shape and up in the air.

Today rue Maître Albert is a street full of art galleries, smart apartments and with a nice little bar. In my days as a child, I would see men fighting with knives, hear lovely Arab music, and watch boys with bikes from my third-floor window, hoping that they would lift their heads and see me. Mother didn't like us to look through the windows. She would say, 'Bats will come in and get caught in your hair,' so we would shut the windows and forget the boys and their bikes. It was through these windows that I lost many a balloon and all my little frogs which had grown from tadpoles. We would get them every springtime in the Bois de Boulogne from little ponds my father would take us to, each little girl with a jar.

My mother always had work tailoring and she always sang when she was sad. She sang about little swallows and it made my sisters and me laugh. Also, Mother always had lollies and surprises in the drawer of her sewing machine for her three little girls that she loved. My father gave her a hard time and I never knew why.

He was very tempestuous and described to me as a villain, but it was my father who took us swimming and to the cinema often, who bought me a bottle of champagne when I was twelve – a rare birthday event for a little girl, my father said. I learned later that my mother was terrified of another pregnancy, and had had an abortion and her three daughters within four years.

Later, when I left for Australia, my father apologised to me for having given a hard time to my mother, who by then had left for New York. She married twice again, to farmers who had little ducks and geese and chickens. Still, she wrote love letters to my father for thirty years, until both died in 1980, within a week of each other, buried and separated by the Atlantic Ocean. My father was the first to die, in the Paris he loved.

During my last holiday with Paulette and Nouzette in Cancale, Bretagne, in 1938, I could feel in my heart that it was the last holiday. There was a terrible war looming. My parents started to have parties for the underground, on the pretence that they were children's parties, and it was my job to look through the windows to see if all was safe outside, down the street. We heard terrible things about concentration camps: our friend Hélène who worked for the underground had thrown herself out of a window on the fourth floor, in front of her little boy tucked up in bed, when the police knocked at her door.

As the German army approached Paris, we left in my father's car. Mother bought us a little live chicken each to hold on to throughout the trip. Petrol ran out, it was the exodus. Italian planes bombarded us and we had to hide in the forest along the road. The forest had traces of people who had left their gas masks and a large amount of heteroclite objects lying about – bits of desperate memories.

Somehow we walked again, leaving our car like everyone else, and found a little village with a kind lord mayor who gave us a tiny house near a small lake, where our one little chicken that we hadn't lost grew rapidly and loved the lake's embankment especially. By then the Germans had invaded the village, and as I went to get some milk from a farm nearby, a German soldier was asking for eggs. The French farmer pretended he didn't understand, so the German soldier bent forward acting like a chook, and mimicked eggs coming out of his bottom; the farmer still not understanding, pretending not to. He and I smiled at each other.

But Paris was our home and we had left everything there, our furniture and possessions, and now we had to go back – to a gloomy city and more hearsay from the Resistance. We heard in 1942 that a big *razzia*, a raid, was inevitable and that we should not be at home on 16th July 1942. My parents didn't know where to go, it was yet another rumour.

Many people had been taken earlier and sent to Drancy, like my poor Aunty Mimi, leaving her baby daughter Dina in a hospital, aged twelve months, and another child, Eveline, who came to us, alone by the Métro for the first time. On 16th July 1942 a wonderful policeman came at 7.30am and instead of taking us said he would come back for us at 11.30am. My parents discussed what to do; my mother sent me for an errand and the thought occurred to me to run away, but where? It was not very noble to leave my family so I returned home feeling despondent. The errand was to the police station, what for I have no idea. A desk and three policemen looking at me is all I remember, a strong image in my brain like a Kafka story – stilted actors. At 11.30am the same policeman who was so remarkable, giving us a second chance to run away, came and said, 'I will return at 1.30pm.' In the meantime, my mother said to my father to go and hide at our neighbour's place and she would go with the children and the policeman. Maybe Father could do something to save us, Mother thought. They literally did not know what to do. When 1.30 came, the policeman took us to the 5th arrondissement's town hall, and from there to the Vélodrome d'Hiver, which was full of people screaming, crying, going insane.

There we were for three days and three nights, sitting on folding seats. The toilets on the first floor were overflowing and I saw a lovely girl from my class lying with her desolate mother in the urine and excrement, stunned like me. At school, the girl, Agnès, always wore a pretty white collar on her *tablier noir* and was the best in the class at mathematics. I went back down to find that my mother was making an incredible speech. I didn't know she could have such a powerful voice and such a strong vocabulary, standing up so little in the big Vélodrome d'Hiver. At night the gigantic shadows would print themselves on walls; shadows of people protesting, gesticulating, like my mother did. When one person stopped, another would start; it went on as if organised, speech after speech. All the sick people were in the middle of the Vélodrome d'Hiver, helpless, screaming, dying. Some *assistantes sociales* tried to help but they were like moths next to a burning light, hopelessly waving their arms, walking in all directions.

Then, after three days and three nights, we were put in buses with policemen surrounding us as far as you could see. I saw a policeman crying, I saw some laughing – no way could you escape. I was sitting near the window, looking at the scene: it was incomprehensible. I still feel ill near a window in a tram or bus. Then we were put in a cattle train and I have no recollection of climbing inside and coming out of it. In vain, I look at films of it. I remember being in it, it was very dark around our feet. There was a beautiful young woman with long blonde hair, holding her teenage son, as tall as her, standing up in the middle of the carriage. While in the train, my mother said to me, 'Madeleine, when the train slows down, try to read the name of the station and I will write it down for Daddy.' After several stations, my mother put the little piece of paper in an envelope, sealed it without a stamp, and when the train slowed down again, Mother gave me the envelope and I slid the envelope through the gaps between the slats of wood on the side of the train.

Someone extraordinary found the envelope, put a stamp on it, and my father received it. From the list of stations my father could deduce that we were headed in the direction of the camp de Pithiviers; from Pithiviers, convoys would take you straight to Auschwitz. My mother and we three girls missed the convoy to Auschwitz, number 16, in August 1942, as we were liberated with fourteen other people on 6th August to go back to Paris. My father, being part of the Jewish Resistance in Paris, had managed to arrange for our release from the camp de Pithiviers.

While still in the camp, I could see men and women and children being separated from each other again. I have no recollection of entering the camp at Pithiviers. I do remember the daily assembly before night-time, outside standing amongst rows of people. The only food was bad beans in water in an empty sardine tin, if you were lucky enough to have one. Throughout the day I walked and walked, praying to the Virgin Mary. A friend of my mother who saw me walking strangely, my hands on my chest praying, asked me many times, 'Why don't you go and play with the children?' I was fourteen and I did notice teenagers writing plays and organising themselves but I did not make the effort of participating or joining them. I just watched them as I walked by, around and around in the camp. The nights were terrible as people would go insane and jump from the top of the bunks. We slept in the same straw bed, the four of us. I can remember the feel of my sisters and my mother in the bed. We were in a lower bunk near the ground, but I have no recollection of them in daytime, as if they didn't exist.

I remember finding a tap and washing myself, near the latrines where there was a line of toilet seats, perhaps twenty of them, made of wood. There was also a kind of villa from which sick children disappeared, we were told. The day we left, our name was called and my mother had to endure a full body search for hidden messages, but I had all the messages – from other people in the camp who hoped we could tell their families where they were – in my socks and underpants as I was not searched, being a child. While my mother was being searched, my sisters and I were already sitting in the cart with the other fourteen people freed. I still feel my anguish waiting for my mother. She appeared eventually and could hardly fit in the full cart as the old horse was starting to pull it, the iron wheels screeching to a halt and then pulling hard again, the horse en route to Pithiviers Station. (Or it may have been Beaune-la-Rolande, as this name is also in my memory.) I still hear the noise of the wheels on the country road and still see the people behind the barbed wire staring at us – that image is forever printed in my mind as it was unbearable to leave them, and at my tender age I felt guilt for the first time.

The cart moving so slowly added to my pain and guilt. I could see all the people fading in the distance but knew their eyes were glued to us, also fading away as the twilight appeared to erase everything – but not what was by then printed in our souls.

We arrived in Paris without wearing the yellow star and after dark. The streets looked like cardboard cut-outs, shadows, with no lights to be seen anywhere. As we passed Notre-Dame, its haunting shape was sinister; we knew we were near home where my father was hoping against hope that we would be freed by his efforts with the Resistance.

A child is strange: as we came to our apartment, I went straight to my parents' bedroom to see if there was another woman in my father's bed. There was not. Next day, my mother went to the hospital to look for Dina, Aunty Mimi's daughter. Dina was still there, so my mother brought her home to live with us. Aunty Mimi later died in Auschwitz. My other little cousin, Eveline, must have gone to join her father, I recall.

At the bed next to Dina in the hospital was another child with her father, a humble man from the country working on the railways – Société Nationale des Chemins de Fer. My mother told him of her plight, just out of the camp de Pithiviers and not knowing what to do or where to go next in the middle of the war. This man, Monsieur Fournier, who worked with the Resistance, told my mother he could help her and her family; there were some good people left in France. He arranged for false papers, a little house in the country, but all the family could not travel together, we could not be noticed.

My sister Salomèe and I were each put in a special family as helpers while all the papers were organised. I was to go first to Paulette in Normandie, who offered to take me at great risk. No sooner did I arrive at Paulette's than I developed scarlet fever, which had been rampant in the camp de Pithiviers. I had missed the sinister villa by a few days, the villa from which sick children never returned. In Normandie I was sent to a nuns' hospital with a terribly high fever and peeling skin. Even though I was so sick, one nun would keep asking me with great insistence if I was really Madeleine Mahdi, born in Tunis (as printed in my false papers), and I was careful to say yes again and again. I can still see her red face close to mine and her piercing eyes, her body in an awkward angle above my bed. Her nun's uniform was familiar but I didn't trust her.

Henri, Paulette's new husband, was very kind. He would come every night with lovely fruits and I felt a little safer when I saw him. I got well and returned to Paulette and Henri's lovely little farm and my pet pig Toto, always clean and clever. I heard him cry once as I came home from the fields – I thought it was a human voice but no, it was Toto being killed for food. I was distraught. The war made people do these things, I knew.

Paulette gave me a big lecture about what to do in case the Germans came to the house. If they did, I was to jump through a window and run into the fields where my favourite jersey cow was and hide in the prickly blackberry bushes. One day, lo and behold, a knock at the door announced a German soldier who had arrived on a motorbike. He asked if Madeleine Mahdi lived in the cottage. Paulette kept her cool and answered, 'Yes.'

'Have you fumigated your house? For we know she was in hospital with scarlet fever.'

'Yes,' answered Paulette again, very coolly. I can still hear the sound of the motorbike in the quiet little village where you only ever heard the church bells ring on the hour. The voice of the German soldier with my name in his mouth is still in my ears. I see myself climbing through the window and running for my life through blackberry bushes and hiding in the fields like an animal. I remember jumping through the window like a thief, jumping out and eventually finding my feet.

Next morning, I was packed up and sent safely to my parents who were hiding in another little village. I don't remember travelling to my parents from Paulette's place but I do remember travelling from Paris to Paulette's village. My mother had made me a little red bonnet so that I would look younger than fourteen – of course it attracted a great deal of attention, but I pretended to be asleep right throughout the trip. When a German soldier came onto the train calling, *'Papiere, papiere!'* ('Papers, papers!') I kept sleeping in the corner, near the door in the train compartment. The soldier didn't see me as I was under his outstretched arm while he looked over the papers people gave him to check. Luck, a fluke, *un hasard extraordinaire*.

Many years later I saw all the lists of convoys to Auschwitz in *French Children of the Holocaust: A Memorial*, by Serge Klarsfeld, a large book full of photographs of children and their parents and toys in happier times. The descriptions of the Vélodrome d'Hiver are exactly how I remember them. The book had been reviewed in the *Bulletin* in 1997 or 1998, but I had trouble getting a copy from booksellers. My friend Serge Thomann, who is a photographer, rang the Paris publishers from my house, and in a week's time the book arrived. (I gave Serge a large charcoal drawing to say thank you.) In the book I found the little girl Rosa Farber who was the daughter of the lady who always told me to play and not walk strangely around and around the camp. In books, the dead are alive, you can caress them, speak to them.

In September 1942 I was back safe with my parents at last, after staying a few days with Monsieur Fournier's brother, the stationmaster. His house was located right on the platform and I could hear the silence between the trains passing by. Monsieur Fournier's job in the Resistance was to put bombs in German trains as they passed through the station, he worked with all the brakes and signals. He was a quiet man. I went to see him work a few times. The brakes looked gigantic to pull back and there was a whole row of them.

The house in the little village where my parents were was beautiful – a big room with two other rooms closed on one side and our two rooms on the opposite side. A primitive kitchen at the end of the big room and there we were to hide until the end of the war. In the garden across from our house was a bungalow where two Spanish men hid. They left before us. I always remember them; they used to smile at me but we rarely saw them. The house was on the main road in the village, whose name I can't remember, and one day as I went out, a car, Citroën-like, passed rapidly, full of German soldiers. My heart sank for a few days with fright.

At the entrance of the next big town stood two German soldiers, each with a gun. They guarded the road and I would ride very fast past them and never stop, down the hill. Coming back, I always had to walk as the hill was too steep, but the two soldiers never stopped me as I was wearing my little red childlike bonnet, trying look younger than my fifteen or sixteen years. When I think of the danger now, I tremble with fear. On my bike, I was going to little farms teaching children to read and write, and bringing home eggs and flour and milk to my family.

For the owner of the house, a stern lady in black, I took her cows to the fields and brought them back. I also used her horse and cart. My father cut wood in the forest, always alone; I would bring him lunch sometimes and watch him cut the wood. He had an axe and sat on a little trunk as he was chopping the wood. My two sisters had to clean the lady's house and didn't like doing it at all. Mother looked after our two little cousins (Eveline had come back to live with us) and her own three daughters and husband. It was a full house.

We thought we were hiding but the entire village knew we were there, as we found out on the first day of spring. It was the ritual in the village to send all the young boys of the town, holding large bunches of lilac, to houses where young girls were growing up. This was a big surprise, and again we were frightened but didn't show it when a swarm of boys knocked on the door and we let them in. I still remember all the boys sitting on the floor along the walls of our big main room and the lilac everywhere on the floor and the heady scent of the carpet of pinkish flowers.

There was a boy who arrived one night on a motorbike, bringing us food, tickets. He took a great liking to my sister Salomèe who was very beautiful, a painter and poet. The boy always disappeared with the Resistance in the forest, at night and daytime. I still cry when I see forests. Forests meant our liberty coming and young people risking their lives for it.

Across the road there was a well where I used to fetch water in a bucket and I lost the full bucket many a time, almost falling into the well if I didn't let go of the bucket in time. My mother, as a child, had seen a lady fall in a well, so I was careful as her story stayed in my mind. She repeated it forcefully. Near the well lived a widow who always came by our open window where my father shaved himself, singing all the sad songs from the First World War and before: 'La Robe Blanche', always people dying in hospital, very poor, and many orphans and dying lovers. We just listened to the songs, gruesome as they were in their most horrid details. But their 1900 tunes were familiar.

There was great tension between my parents. They slept in different rooms and we had to find spiders to put in the soup my mother would cook for my father. Bizarre. Five little girls all look-ing for spiders that my mother hoped would make my father sick. One day, I went outside the house as I heard a lot of voices and cars, and saw a big truck full of American soldiers throwing us packets of cigarettes and chewing-gum. Ah! The joy! A vision. Liberation had arrived and the most terrible thing happened to our family in the next few days. My father became very fierce and kept saying that he would cut off my mother's head as soon as we got back to Paris. My mother was petrified and one day, when I didn't let my father enter my mother's room, I attacked him with my foot, you know where. I received *un coup de poing* on my stomach, passing out after seeing three stars, my bladder emptying itself everywhere on the floor where I lay unconscious.

I was very frightened for my mother and went to see Madame Fournier to ask for help. Alas, instead of getting a psychiatrist or a doctor, she sent two policemen and my poor father was arrested. A court case ensued, Madame Fournier attended. We went back to Paris without a father, telling everybody that he was coming home soon. But he was put in jail in Paris, where my mother and sisters went every day to take him food. He never told my mother when he was getting out of jail, and after a month a family friend, Madame Brainne, told us that our father was staying with her and would like to see us. During our childhood, whenever my mother left my father and took us with her, Madame Brainne was always there to help save the marriage and Mother would return every time. This time my mother said yes again, and I was to ask for for-giveness, which I did: *'Papa, je te demande pardon.'*

When my father came home, his black hair had turned white and he walked with a cane. Soon he was as good as gold, no more bad temper and threats, but with a broken heart and haunted night and day by his incarceration. But Mother still wanted to go to America, her first dream, so in 1946 I helped my parents to divorce and my mother to find her brother in New York, and twenty-five years after she'd first tried to go to America, she finally got there, with the help of my future husband, Georges.

On our return to Paris in 1945, I went back to school. I was always writing plays and my professor of literature would put my plays on. Remarkable. I was impatient to get on with life and noticed I was not good in mathematics, so I quit school. I was troublesome to my mother, who promptly took me to a doctor who decided to give me electric shocks at the back of my head. After two sessions, I realised my mother and the doctor were not right, and refused to get more electric shocks. I put my age up, and on the advice of another doctor decided to enrol myself as a *monitrice* in an orphanage run by Oeuvre de Secours aux Enfants, a Jewish organisation who had saved children during the war. I got the job and at seventeen, pretending to be eighteen, I started my life in Saint-Quay-Portrieux, where the orphanage was, on the seaside *en Bretagne*.

I made friends in the little town with a family who all played chamber music, and I would go and listen. It was unforgettable. Often I was the only audience member. The father was my friend, a doctor I had gone to one day after seeing an enormous pink worm, fifteen inches long and very fat, in my poop. No big worm ever came again but I have never forgotten my surprise as I saw the worm. *Le ver solitaire*. The doctor became my good friend and I became a lover of chamber music – sweet life, sweet doctor.

There was a boy in Saint-Quay-Portrieux called François, an accordion player who had a beautiful girlfriend during the day but would meet me at night in a tree outside my bedroom window, when everyone in the orphanage was asleep. He would suckle my nipples, tell me sweet things in the sea air, and I would go back to my bedroom via a large branch near my open window on the first floor, agile like a monkey. That's how far my sexual education went. During the day, the other girlfriend would stare at me, her two eyes like arrows to kill me.

One day a big commotion happened in the director's office at the orphanage. Georges Mora was to come down from Paris and visit the two orphanages by the seaside. Georges was Chef de Bureau of the OSE. He came with three friends, three very interesting women who in turn stared at me. Adrienne, whose boyfriend was a man with one hand (the other was eaten by a tiger when he was on a safari); Charlotte, who later married the writer Manès Sperber; and Mireille, who was available. One day, entering the director's office, I heard a voice saying, 'Is there anyone who likes a game of ping-pong?' It was Georges' voice. Having never played ping-pong before, I still offered myself for a game at lunchtime. I quickly went to buy myself a pair of espadrilles and presented myself to this charming man to play ping-pong for a little while. He wore grey pants and a white jumper and I thought he would make a good father for the children I wanted to produce – thinking that, to be a complete woman, you had to have children first. A peculiar thought for a young virgin. I was crazy about babies and would go to every chemist, take all the pamphlets with pictures of babies on them and cut them out to hold them better.

Georges Mora came every month and always brought his lovely gang of brilliant girls. We would all go dancing at night. I danced cheek to cheek with Georges. Georges did ask me about François and I was amazed he had heard of him; the gossip probably had come from people who saw me going to watch François play the accordion and saw the attention he paid me at intervals. (I don't remember the songs they played, only one, *'La Mer'*, by Charles Trénet, but was asked if I would like to play the drums. I didn't take up the offer.)

After a year in Saint-Quay-Portrieux, I decided to go back to Paris to join the Ecole d'Education Par le Jeu et l'Art Dramatique (EPJD), a theatre school. I had seen an advertisement in the papers and the list of teachers read: Jean Louis Barrault, Marcel Marceau, Mytho Bourgoin, Jean Vilar, Roger Blin, Jean-Marie Conti, Jean Paulhan, Etienne Decroux, the very best in the world of theatre at that time. What attracted me also was that the EPJD had been born during the war and went from school to school making sure the children wouldn't be brainwashed by the invaders and the Vichy government, and making plays with the children.

I had money for the initial fees, and after my small savings dwindled, Georges Mora kindly paid them. My father didn't like Georges Mora at first, my mother adored him at once. Paulette and Georges didn't become friends either. I liked Georges' beautiful hands, his voice, and the way he wore his gabardine raincoat on his arm as he waited for me at different *rendez-vous* all over Paris, especially in restaurants. Sometimes I would wait for him in lovely intimate bars with a pianist playing languorous music. Georges often had OSE meetings in rue Spontini.

Older male friends of Georges used to giggle and tease him about me but I wouldn't really know why. Sometimes they would give me pocket money, which I would not refuse. I thought that maybe I ought to be deflowered and then they would not tease us. A virgin is sexless, neither boy nor girl – this was a seventeenth-century belief in Mexico. Georges refused and thought that we had to be married first. I was slightly humiliated, and from what

I understood of his friends' teasing, to them I was only a child at eighteen. Georges was fifteen years older than me.

But we did get married, in December 1947, and I lost my virginity at Barbizon, in a little hotel in a treasure of a village where many painters had come to paint the landscape from 1836. Later that century, great painters met to form a common front against the art institute in Paris, which was so academic, and gave birth to the magic oak trees of Barbizon – the origins of impressionism and l'Ecole de Barbizon. There is a beautiful book, *Les Peintres et leur école Barbizon*, by André Parinaud. In 1994 I arrived in Cannes for the film festival, having been invited by my son Philippe and his wife Pamela. The book on the Barbizon school had just been released and I bought and read it ravenously. A good coincidence.

Back in December 1947, after the Barbizon *dépucelage*, we realised that we had not taken photographs of the wedding, which had been a very big wedding in rue Spontini in Paris, at the head office of the OSE, so we put on our wedding clothes again and went to have our photos taken, quite happily. There must be people who have photos of my wedding but I don't. A sad omen.

The Cold War was a threat in the fifties and I was terrified of living through another war in Paris with my husband and my first child, Philippe, who was born in 1949. I wanted to leave Paris as soon as possible. We had three choices: Casablanca, which Georges knew well and loved; Saigon, where he was offered a job by his brother-in-law; or Melbourne, which was my obsession.

I wanted to go to Melbourne as I had read about it in a novel I was not allowed to read but did, *Scènes de la vie de bohème* by Henri Murger. I read it in secret at sixteen. My father thought that I should not read books that might excite me. In it was a lovely young photographer who was part of a gang of artists, musicians, writers, singers and painters, and this photographer made regular trips to Melbourne to make his fortune. He would then lose it all and return to Paris and his gang, and then go back to Melbourne. His name was Antoine Fauchery and his work is in Melbourne at Museum Victoria. (Later, I met a charming woman, Diane Reilly, who co-wrote the text for Antoine Fauchery's book, *Sun Pictures of Victoria: The Fauchery–Daintree Collection, 1858*, a book that I acquired with much delight.)

At school, my first reading book had featured a kangaroo who worked as a postman and he had letters in his pouch and a cap on his head. This was my first picture of faraway Australia. That reading book is imprinted in my mind because it had lovely running writing, pictures in colour, and the word *feuille*, which seemed so mysterious because the 'i' before two 'l's changes the sound of the 'l's, making them sound like 'yew', as in 'you'. If I had not been so intrigued by the shape of the word *feuille*, I might not have remembered the kangaroo.

I convinced Georges to go
to Melbourne.

MY MELBOURNE

eorges was sad to leave Paris, I was ready to tackle my new life. Australia had endless publicity in the Paris newspapers, showing pictures of the desert I loved – odd that it didn't show cities to encourage migrants. We flew to New York first, after a stop in England as the plane had to be repaired. Because there wasn't room for a whole planeload of people in the hotels, the airline put us up in a beautiful castle and I slept in Anne Boleyn's bed. Philippe cried all night. The room was long and dark with a large carved wooden bed.

In New York we stayed three months to see my mother, Georges to see his sister Edith and her family, then a hop and a jump over the Rocky Mountains, which gave me a terrible fright as our plane was small and we bumped around, up and down. We stopped in Tahiti for three days where I had a very painful, stiff neck. We eventually landed at Essendon airport in Melbourne and were later deposited outside the National Gallery in Swanston Street, at an airport arrival and departure pick-up point. A sign. It was July 1951, I was twenty-three with just two phrases in English: 'the sky is blue' and 'the fountain is in the garden'. I also had a two-volume English–French dictionary which my father had bought for me when I was twelve, for my *Certificat d'Etudes*. Georges could speak perfect English as his work in Paris as a patent agent had involved monthly trips to London.

Our first abode in Melbourne was in St Kilda Road, then Gatehouse Street in Parkville where Sidney Nolan and John Sinclair had a studio once. Badly advised, we went to the outer suburb of McKinnon for six months. I kept fainting in the butcher's shop, but the butcher was very polite about it all. The smell of the meat was too strong for me.

On the plane from New York, an inquisitive paediatrician called Molly Douglas had taken an interest in us. She was intrigued with my way of handling Philippe – as though he were a little adult. At the time she was taking care of the architect Roy Ground's little daughter, Victoria. We went once to their house in Mt Eliza. I was impressed to see a blackboard on the wall for the little girl to work on and play with chalk of various colours.

Molly Douglas had a friend called Colin Wainwright; my husband and I fell in love with him and he came to live with us for a while. He was sheer joy and drank an enormous amount of tea. He was so flamboyant, and a good friend. He was friendly with Michael Miller, the brother of Tatlock Miller, the royal photographer whose album of photographs I have guarded all these years.

Michael had a dress shop in Fitzroy Street, St Kilda, and a carpet snake; his great joke was to let the snake slide into the cubicles while ladies were trying dresses on. The ladies would scream and run out into the street in their underwear. He also had birds in cages that he would let loose. They would poop on the dresses and everywhere else. Riots of laughter all the time. Michael also had a big cockatoo that I inherited and called Mr Jesus. It would wake up the entire street in McKinnon screeching, 'Mirka, Mirka.' We were not exactly popular at number 6, Elindale Avenue.

Colin had a friend, Mrs Bentwich, a lady of a certain age. She had been the mistress of General Monash and was still wearing beautiful clothes made in Vienna. She was great company. We went once to see the daffodil fields outside Melbourne. In those days we had an empty van, and to make Mrs Bentwich comfortable I put a large *fauteuil* and Colin and John Spencer, another friend, held the *fauteuil* so it wouldn't slide downhill. John Spencer had arrived at my studio one day from England. He had come to Australia to make up his mind about whether or not to become a Catholic priest. Soon, I introduced him to Edith, a French girl who lived in Melbourne. After all sorts of incidents, *péripéties*, they married each other, went to London and had a swarm of children. Charles Blackman would sometimes see her and give us news of her family life when he came back to Melbourne from England.

One very hot summer day in McKinnon our neighbours complained because they said our grass at the front was too high. I was tired of cutting it and told Colin of my plight. He said, 'Can I have your turpentine?' then asked me for my matches, and in no time had thrown the turpentine on the high dry grass, lit the match, *et voilà!* The grass had gone.

I longed to have a studio where I could do some dressmaking and painting and not be so isolated. But where to find one? Again, I told Colin of my wish and he said, 'I know where there is one, in town at 9 Collins Street, but it is owned by a photographer and he will want money for a bond.'

It took six months and my husband's diplomacy to finally get the studio. Mrs Lina Bryans, a painter of note, also wanted the studio. I didn't know her history then, or the studio's, but later when I did I realised she must have been sad to miss out on the studio. It had been the studio of Arthur Streeton, Tom Roberts, Frederick McCubbin, Sir John Longstaff, Jane Sutherland and Ola Cohn. So many people had created the atmosphere through the years. Sometimes, when I am reading, I find mentions of 9 Collins Street during the 1930s and 1940s. (This period is discussed in the book *Max Meldrum and Associates* by Peter and John Perry.)

I felt glued to the studio on the first visit. Somehow I felt I already knew its history and sensed my future there. Georges, Philippe and I went many times to talk to Mr Davis, who owned and lived in the studio. He was an old and difficult man. One day I went alone with Philippe, and the next day Georges was to go by himself to seal the deal. Mr Davis didn't approve of the way I was educating my child; Philippe had found a long stick and given Mr Davis a black eye with it. I didn't dare tell my husband and I didn't even prepare him for the story. On the next day, Mr Davis opened his door to be greeted by Georges, who saw his big black eye and said, 'Oh! You must have had a good party last night.'

'No', said Mr Davis, 'it was your son who knocked my eye with a wooden stick.' This event made the whole deal take longer, but in mid-1952 we finally settled in the studio for the next fifteen years.

As a child in Paris I always stared at a print Paulette had on the wall of her dining room. The painting, by a French artist, represented a studio at the turn of the century in Paris. There was a violinist, someone at the piano, a man smoking sitting on a high stool, a couch with two lovers *enlacés*, and one poet sitting in a melancholy state, his head in his hands.

Number 9 Collins Street had that mood and soon got its painters, poets, musicians and philosophers: everyone who was interesting in Melbourne. And its lovers, of course. In those days, no one lived in the city, so journalists, politicians and friends soon made a habit of coming for breakfast, often twenty people, to start the day. It was so stimulating and was a good education for me to discover the quality of all these people and the beating heart of Melbourne.

Doc Evatt would come during the day; he loved black ink. I would put some on a piece of paper, he would fold it; sometimes he would put the black ink on the paper, we would fold the paper in turns. Every time we opened it, the ink design was that of a judge's wig and we laughed and laughed. He loved speaking about the United Nations and being its president, voting for human rights and the State of Israel in Paris, 1948. He played the organ very well, an old musical instrument I had bought at Tye's furniture shop in Bourke Street, which is now long gone.

The big excitement for me was to go to Georges department store in Collins Street to buy lovely material. I used to make my own clothes, which is easy when you have a small waist and bosoms like two little peaches. Since Georges Mora spoke English very well, he had taken a few professional dressmaking lessons so that he could then teach me. But I had a better idea. I would wait until Georges was asleep and I would open up his suit sleeves so that I could see how to do it and then close them again before Georges woke up in the morning. Once, I got a lady into her dress that I had just made, but when in it she could not move her arms. She laughed kindly, and brought croissants to the next fitting when I had improved the armholes.

Georges of Collins Street commissioned me to make dickies, *plastrons* in French, detachable shirt fronts. When I was pregnant with my second son, William, and could not bend any more to fix hems on ladies' dresses, I also made collars and cuffs with lace and beads sewn onto velvet.

One day, a charming man called Mr Black who was working at Georges and who was very intrigued by my good taste, invited me to a party. He had been very kind to me earlier on by sending me customers when I lived in McKinnon and was trying my hand at dressmaking. A woman called Helen, who was to marry Len French, then still a promising young painter, was my assistant. The party was in St Kilda Road in a big mansion, the home of a well-known Melbourne family, the Rudducks. Irene Mitchell – the soul of St Martins Theatre, which was at the time an avant-garde theatre – and many of her actors were in one of the rooms. I was wearing a beautiful flat, black, shiny straw hat that I had bought with Georges in avenue de l'Opéra in Paris. It had a red silk rose attached to it. That night, I threw it into the fire (a good bit of acting, I thought). I sat next to a man on a sofa and we talked to each other late into the night. My hostess, Mrs Rudduck, was fascinated, as usually this fine man hardly spoke to anyone. His name was John Sinclair and he was the music critic for the *Herald* at the time. We spoke of Paris, its streets and monuments, and he knew everything and had never been to the city. He went later and I saw him off at the airport, grinning with envy. I can still see him climbing the little stairs up to the plane.

The very next morning the telephone rang and a little voice

with an unforgettable tone – soft, persistent, rare – came from very far away. It was the voice of Sunday Reed, to whom John Sinclair had described me, and would I make a dress for her? Yes, I said, most interested. I chose some very fine white linen, *batiste*, and the dress was so lovely that Sunday hung it on her bedroom wall. She never wore it, choosing to look at it instead.

John Reed came to collect the dress and gave me a cheque. He looked extremely handsome in my dark studio with his white hair. We stared at one another, our eyes had a real encounter as we stared at each other profoundly. It was the beginning of a long friendship and great projects were achieved, such as the Museum of Modern Art in Melbourne, which came about as a result of the revival of the Contemporary Art Society in the studio. The revival, the first meeting of many, filled up the studio with artists, chock-a-block. I remember Danila Vassilieff praising John Reed. I remember Ian Sime being extremely eloquent. John Reed also made a speech. We were making history and it was all about painting and sculpture, the art that we all loved so passionately.

Soon we spent every weekend at Heide with John and Sunday; the library was a haven, full of French books. Later, when I was fifty years old, Sunday gave me Rimbaud's *Correspondance, 1888–1891*, and she had had the book since 1928. She wrote something very moving for me on a little piece of blue paper in her voluptuous handwriting. Sweeney, her little adopted son, delivered the book to me on 18th March 1978.

During the week, when they came to the studio, John and Sunday would bring rare roses, eggs, cream, asparagus, fruit and books. It was very poetic, romantic and special, especially the chervil I had loved in France. Sometimes, Sweeney would come and stay in the studio with a bag packed with lovely clothes.

I remember in particular the good jumpers in soft colours. Once when he came, I turned the studio into a fortress and gave Philippe, William and Sweeney water pistols and they would shoot water at whoever came to the studio. I was very popular with the three boys. The children also painted Aboriginals on the walls, in the little sitting room.

Sweeney was extremely beautiful, a wild child, very intelligent. He had been born to Joy Hester and Albert Tucker. There was a kind of aura around Sweeney. He was quick with words. He managed to tame Cleopatra, a white feral cat with big red eyes from the Fitzroy Gardens which sometimes came to see Napoléon, our black cat. Sweeney had a way with cats as John and Sunday had at the time a cattery with almost forty cats. They all cried loudly, they were Burmese and Siamese and pissed on all the paintings standing in the corridor. They also had a Jersey cow, the same as my cow Bella during the war. My Bella was killed by a bomb in the French meadow where I once hid from a German soldier on a motorbike.

Soon, we built a house at the seaside town of Aspendale for the weekends. Our house was built by the architect Peter Burns, and Georges found a house next door to ours where a wild woman lived with all the windows nailed shut and at least thirty dogs chained up in the house. It was *épouvantable* to witness such a scene, maltreated and sad dogs. With Georges' gentle talk to the lady and the RSPCA the dogs were put in kennels. The house was bought and demolished to build another that was designed by David McGlashan. There, for ten years, great parties and dramas were had. This was John and Sunday's house, next to ours. In the old house, before it was demolished, I remember Albert Tucker in a bed against the wall in a spartan room, looking like a Christ as I popped my head through the door, which is amazing as I can't resist a man in bed.

During the early 1960s, Albert took photographs at Aspendale of all of us and our visitors.

The children could get some good fresh air and swim and have fun. Life in the studio was a little restricted for a family, even though there was no end to entertainment by the endless *défilé* of visitors who often stayed the night downstairs, sleeping in front of the fireplace in winter and talking right through the night, sometimes keeping us awake. When I asked my children once what aspect of their childhood they loved most, they all said, 'We loved all the people coming to the house.'

We also had many Contemporary Art Society exhibition opening and closing parties at the studio, or ending at the studio. I remember Hephzibah Menuhin opening a show, Sir Ralph Richardson, Barrett Reid, the composer Dorian le Galienne, it was sheer poetry. Dorian le Galienne wrote the music for a film by Tim Burstall on John Perceval's angels. One of our treasured visitors was Laurence Hope – a sombre painter, but very romantic. His father would often come to see us when in town from Queensland to thank my husband and me for being so kind to his son. Laurence would go to all the parties in town, for there were many in the fifties and sixties, and would tell my boys, who always asked, if he had caught a girl. They had a secret language they used to talk about this. Laurence also came to Aspendale where we had great conversations, visitors and endless games of chess. Laurence was a great raconteur and took lots of photographs, which have recently been sold to the National Library in Canberra.

The story we loved the most was when Charles Blackman and Laurence Hope, who were friends, got a job in Brisbane washing the dishes in a large hospital, and Laurence, wearing a white blouse, was taken for a doctor, but was eventually caught by a patient.

There were all sorts of stories from that hospital which made you cry or laugh: the slippery floor, slippery piles of plates which crashed to the floor. Laurence was a good storyteller. In summer he always wore loose shorts and we could see his jewels dangling out of his shorts, to the great delight of all. He married later and had a son.

Gareth Sansom, who later became the Dean of the Victorian College of the Arts, also came often, to the joy of my children who one summer played endlessly with big carrots in their swimsuits, showing off and acting out erotic scenes as I took pictures. Gareth was very helpful to my son Philippe when he was a teenager making films, driving the car as Philippe was filming.

If lunch was at my place we had to have afternoon tea or dinner at the Reeds'. We alternated all the time, both houses were like beehives, gossip galore, and there were touches of *Le Grand Meaulnes* (a novel I love by the French writer Alain-Fournier) with many a visitor and their mysteries. Big drama when Charles Osborne went to London to a great career in the literary world and I didn't know whose lover he was, Barrie Reid's or Philip Jones'. That day I came to the conclusion that men's love for each other was perhaps stronger than between a man and a woman, but I was ignorant and bewildered, being myself in a pure, deep involvement with another man at that time (my husband's description of it).

It was lovely when George Baldessin, a great printmaker and sculptor, came for afternoon tea and the conversation centred around what it was like to be a vegetarian, which Sunday Reed was. Sunday thought George Baldessin was divine; anyhow, I whispered in his ear to ask Sunday how she could be a vegetarian when she fed her cats with rabbits and chickens, and so he did and all Hell and Leather came about. Sunday left the table – chaos – I felt very wicked and so did George Baldessin, but it is good to create a little chaos during a peaceful afternoon tea in summertime. Makes your blood run fast.

When the Percevals came back from France and England, John and Sunday lent them their house at Aspendale in exchange for a lovely painting. I think it was of Reginald Ansett in a helicopter flying over Aspendale on his way to Sorrento or Portsea, which he did most often on Sundays. The Perceval girls, Alice, Tessa and Winkie, were very protective of Philippe, William and Tiriel – who was born in 1958 – if the big boys attacked my little boys. The girls were very fierce. They looked lovely, fresh from France, all sunburnt and *demoiselles en fleurs*. Joy Hester came with her two other children, Peregrine and Fern, to mingle with our children.

There is a picture I took of the children sitting at a table in the sea, with an umbrella protecting them from the sun. It must have been a hot day. Sometimes I would put my cat in a basket in the sea to cool the cat. Another summer in the sixties, again both houses were full of guests. In mine was a man who right throughout the night went to visit a lady next door at the Reeds'. He was courting her. He would come back slightly tipsy and trip over the wooden steps as he returned. I would lie in my bed and laugh like an imbecile. It probably happened three or four times during the night. As daylight came, I got up to observe the sea, the beach, the sunrise. It was hazy, the boats on the sea seemed to be in the sky as the horizon disappeared in the haze. Everyone was asleep, and as I came back to my house I tripped over on our wooden steps and lifted my big toenail completely. Excruciating pain. I was not laughing any more, even though it was funny. I was punished for laughing about my friend tripping over through the night. He did marry the lovely woman he was courting. Sweeney took me to the doctor as I was fainting with the pain.

Another day, Tiriel jumped on a piece of glass hiding in the sand and I fainted again as William carefully took the glass out of Tiriel's knee. We all went to the doctor and I fainted yet again in the doctor's room. I faint easily, which is most embarrassing.

John Olsen came for the day once. Martin Sharp was there, and our dear friend Harry Youlden who always took photographs, that day using Robert Whitaker's camera. Robert was wearing lovely tight short shorts and I couldn't help seeing an air ticket popping out of his pocket as I was lusting over his tight, round bottom. Divine. He was so happy, he was going to London to photograph The Beatles, and Brian Epstein had given him the air ticket. We were amazed and so pleased for Bob, who was starting his fabulous career. There is a picture of Georges and myself that day at Aspendale, taken by Bob, in his book called *The Unseen Beatles*. There are also lovely short films made by my son Philippe at the Reeds' at Aspendale, with Vassilieff's sculptures, I remember, starring William and Sweeney. Precious memories.

I am a listener and watcher: I could see Georges and John Olsen talking intensely to each other. Letters followed. On that day, Olsen made a portrait of Georges. When it was time to sit down for dinner, I painted my face in the bathroom with zinc cream and mascara. I came out to join the table and my cat hissed with fright. Later, a picture of me taken at the time was on the cover of *Oz* magazine. You can't do better than that on a Sunday afternoon, and it makes me think of Marcus Aurelius Antoninus: 'Time is like a river made up of the events which happen, and its current is strong; no sooner does anything appear than it is swept away, and another comes in its place, and will be swept away too.'

And so it was at Aspendale. Many people came to our house as it was on the way to Portsea. Sometimes people I didn't know came, and off to the beach we all went. John and Sunday came to the beach when the sun came down, was setting and was still, and there were no more shadows. John loved the colourful bikinis. Sunday always had a knowing smile when love's intrigues were displayed, and you could feel in the air passion in all shapes and forms. One Christmas, Sunday bought me a toy boat with a motor attached to it, which would start up by itself during the night and wake up the entire household and guests. That summer, all the children had a little motor they were crazy about. Sunday, Mary Perceval and I would cry right through the summer, we laughed as much as we cried. Sunday would say to me, 'I can't have power over you.' Why, I wondered, did she have such ideas, such thoughts? It left me feeling odd, being a free being.

One summer an invasion of crickets came and one lodged itself in little Alice Perceval's long blonde hair. We could not find the cricket. Alice squeaking as a child would. Once, the sea covered the beach and left a kind of lake; we turned two old wooden drawers into boats as they floated so well. One for Alice and one for Tiriel. The older children played for hours pushing the drawers with the two little sailors. I took photographs. One night, the time came for an artistic display; Mary and I, each holding our littlest child, walked as a performance stark naked to please our male audience and Sunday and Sweeney, round and round in the courtyard. Very daring. We walked like a tribe, pure theatre I thought we were having, but it made no sense, just a *tableau vivant*. A *poème live*.

Other summers, other scenes. Joy Hester wild, screaming sentences so terrible they would make the head of the Medusa a pleasure to look at. At Joy's feet, in my poor little house, Sweeney lay on the floor in a foetal position. No sound from him.

Later that same summer the Blackmans came. There were too many car toys on the floor, making Barbara trip, but she never fell over. And the lovely day John Reed rented a motorboat to go out onto the bay for a few hours. Alice screamed right through the length of our sea voyage. John Reed got the leather belt in his face as he started the motor and kept going without a grimace. I have photos from that event, but it is so long ago, they are fading away. 'Le Bateau Ivre' – a poem by Rimbaud that we loved. Also, I remember the little blue cushions in the train from Sydney to Melbourne as I came back from a holiday in Queensland with my sons. John and Sunday had reserved a big suite at the Wentworth Hotel to meet us and then we all went back to Melbourne together.

Once, at Aspendale, we were all sitting at the table, twelve of us at least, and instead of asking one of the men to help me carry the heavy pot of soup from the stove to the table, I went to get the pot and dropped it on the floor. It was fresh pea soup that Georges had made. On the floor was our dinner, an anticlimax if ever there was one. Total consternation for me and some of my guests. Another wild night, as Mary Perceval was looking for Alice who had disappeared on the beach, John Perceval decided to prepare the salad, which was looking beautiful in one of his great pottery dishes he had created and given to me. I took a photo of John, who, instead of putting salt into the salad, used washing powder by mistake. We could not eat it. What seemed like hours later, Mary found Alice on the beach – far away towards Mordialloc. It was a drama.

Near the stove I had pierced many holes in the floor, and when the floor was swept all the sand fell through the holes and under the house. My invention was much admired by everybody. That summer, Napoléon our cat opened a big lizard's tummy and all the baby lizards ran away for the children to marvel at, such a wonder.

John Perceval was starting to be very ill with his alcohol-related disease, and sometimes I would put him in my bed to warm him up with my body. None of us realised how ill he was. I think the mornings were bad for John as he drank rum and whiskey early in the morning and Georges Mora was very worried about it, a sign of illness to come. Illness did come to John, terribly, and we did get some help, but this is another story – a long story.

The days would go on with many chores to attend to and paintings to be done – and fun to be had, and lunches, dinners and arvo teas, *sans scènes*. One day John Perceval had to go to town and Mary put a very lovely pink *ruban* on John's erect *fascinum* so that he would come home with it and not do any hanky-panky with anyone else. We were all beautiful children pretending to be grown-ups. Winters at Aspendale were quieter. I just went to swim in my fur coat so the icy wind wouldn't go through the fur as I came out of the water.

Back in town, the parties at 9 Collins Street always started with a brick thrown at the windows of the studio by a cranky lady who was a neighbour. Then Allan Swinburn, a Melbourne personage, would come often with a nice young sailor in uniform, then the music would start, then a few people, David and Hermia Boyd; then the studio was full of people dancing to rock-and-roll, often until the morning, when I would cook a duck to please John Perceval. People from Sydney would come down, lovers to Melbourne girls we thought we knew. It was hearsay, but proven to be right later many a time. Most of us were existentialists and well read; we were sure of ourselves in the cultural desert that Australia was then, the place I knew from newspapers in Paris.

As well as the legendary brick that was thrown through our window, the police would come and I would usually speak to them about art, as they did not know what it was, particularly if they saw nude sculptures in my open art books, or if I happened to dance in my shorts (my black ones from Saint-Tropez), and a black brassière from Paris. The policemen were puzzled, and were always nice as they didn't know what to do with such happy people in the middle of the city of Melbourne. The parties would often last three days and three nights. One day I really wanted everyone to leave, so I said that one of my children upstairs had the mumps. You should have seen everybody running away into the Fitzroy Gardens. In panic, especially the men. I remember Julius Kane was the fastest to leave. Poor man, he suicided later. I still have one of his plaster sculptures.

The Fitzroy Gardens was where William and Tiriel learned to walk and where Philippe made his first films, at the pond, aged eleven. The pond where we went fishing for yabbies for dinner. The synopsis of the film was: Tiriel pushes William into the pond. William knows about the yabbies and jumps out of the pond so fast that it is almost unbelievable on the film. But it is filmed. Once, we had a children's party and I thought that at a certain time we would go to the Fitzroy Gardens and feed the possums with bananas. I didn't know if it would work and there we were, twenty small children and myself, very quiet at the bottom of the big tree, waiting, each holding up a banana, when a possum came down and ate a banana. It was enchanting and we all went back to the studio having been ravished by a little possum in the city of Melbourne. Now I have many possums in my *petit jardin*. They eat all my avocados and then go away to drive my cat to distraction, then they tackle my nectarine tree which came from Shepparton.

A real poet with white luminous hair, even though he was very young, was in Melbourne on Friday 6th February 1962. Geoffrey Dutton rang and knocked at my door, as he could hear my footsteps, but unlike Little Red Riding Hood, I didn't open the door and a poem appeared under my door. A poem I cherish always, the last two lines of which read 'When the mind has seen/What might have been.' *Hélas*, I am still a coward when it comes to love-courage.

My Paris was slowly fading away. The more I tried to grasp my new language, English, the more my French behaved like a slippery eel in my mouth. I think in French, it seems, and write in English. Therefore, my prose is most peculiar but alive; sometimes people laugh at my turn of phrase and this pleases me. Mallarmé said once that the sound of a word is more important than its meaning sometimes. I often wonder if I would have been the same person had I not left Paris. Would my work be different? Once, Barbara Blackman, by sheer coincidence, got in contact with a blind poet we had known in Paris. Her name was Angèle Vannier, she often was on the radio, a kind of Edith Piaf of poetry, used by men. Often I thought of my friend Catherine Sauvage who became a great singer and was with me at the EPJD when we were teenagers.

Every city has great artists; we just have to find them and love them at our own peril, if we dare, for they must go, leaving behind our youth and memories that daydreamings are made of. They are *étoiles filantes* in the sky, shooting stars on hot summer nights.

MY ReSTauRaNTS, 1954–1970

s John Reed was
leaving my studio at 9 Collins Street after yet another party where
my husband and I had fed our visitors with good food, wine, music
and great conversation, a thought came to me to open a little café. I
told John on the doorstep and straight away he said that it was not
a good idea, and he left and I was very perplexed, but stuck to my
idea. Georges, who was very miserable being a director of a noodle
factory, loved my idea, so we told our friends, found a place in Exhibition Street, and soon everybody was ready to help decorate the
little place.

The sculptor Julius Kane offered to build the bar, and Dawn
and Ian Sime offered to paint the walls and ceiling, perched on a
scaffold. Clifford Last created a beautiful exotic lamp to be hung
from the ceiling. John Reed came around to the idea, and with
Sunday's good instincts for fun and games to come, offered to lend

us some important paintings by Albert Tucker, Arthur Boyd, John Perceval, Danila Vassilieff, and others. Laurence Hope painted a Woolloomooloo painting, quite large, to be hung behind the bar for all to see. It had a dark background, people in streets and little houses – a Sydney-like and romantic work. The paintings were for sale but there were no buyers to be found. They were a hundred pounds each and sold later for thousands of dollars.

The idea was to charge for food and coffee, but few people among our friends had money. Slowly a clientele who had money came, and we kept feeding those who had no money all the same. I became the cook, with Madame Authier as my second chef. Strictly French food. I was fascinated by my husband always buying the right amount of everything. There was no waste, just good planning. Young students, boys and girls, came in their school uniforms, and Georges thought it was a good education for them to see paintings, drink coffee or hot chocolate and eat *baba au rhum* or croissants, and talk to or watch fascinating people. Soon my good cooking and good looks attracted people from the city for lunch, dinner and supper. My cooking was simple: *blanquette de veau*, *boeuf bourguignon*, *rôti de porc*, *rôti de boeuf*, and Georges' favourite dish, lobster mayonnaise. The mayonnaise was handmade by me and we served the best fillet steak in town. Far away from Melbourne, in the suburbs, there was a French bakery who delivered to us croissants and baguettes and lovely frog cakes and *éclairs au chocolat*, which my little boys loved.

Jean Sablon, who was a very famous French singer, was in town and kindly offered to launch the little café at 183 Exhibition Street, close to Her Majesty's Theatre and the Comedy Theatre, in the heart of Melbourne. Jean Sablon came every night after his show with his producer, who was slightly appalled at having to listen to the *histoires cochonnes* that I loved and laughed about. Not many other people around us understood them because the stories were in French. Soon we were to meet the actors of all the plays coming to town – *Annie Get Your Gun, South Pacific, Paint Your Wagon* – and the ballets and operas. As time passed, we also had to say goodbye many times to friends we had just made. I started to understand at twenty-five years of age that life was about parting, meeting and parting. Zoe Caldwell came to say goodbye. Leo McKern came to say goodbye. John Constable the designer came to say goodbye. Many set designers came to say goodbye and it seemed that everybody went overseas to try their luck. Many succeeded and many were never the same when they came back.

The Mirka Café was packed at night-time with all the theatre spectators looking for a place to eat or have a coffee after the shows. Georges had the idea to serve little open sandwiches, very tasty, that another lady specially prepared, and they were the rage after the theatre, to eat with coffee. Georges bought a coffee machine to make the first cappuccinos, at the same time as Pellegrini's. I didn't really know how to use it, and one day, as John and Sunday entered the café, I let go of the handle and it knocked me on my chin, I nearly fainted with pain and embarrassment. John and Sunday never forgot it and often spoke of it.

Soon, in the room upstairs, the Contemporary Art Society meetings started and it gave the café an air of *conspiration*. The aim was to organise exhibitions of paintings, and especially one in 1954 for the Royal Visit, in opposition to the one organised by the city elders in the Melbourne Town Hall. We had ours in my studio at 9 Collins Street and a great success it was, as the CAS had the best painters. One day, as I was guarding the show, the great Albert Namatjira came with two detectives. I gave a catalogue to

Namatjira and he promptly gave it to one of the detectives. Namatjira stayed a long time, looking at each painting thoughtfully. We also had shows at the Mirka Café. Cliff Pugh sold a portrait of Georges Mora holding a cup with my name on it. A John Passmore was sold to the National Gallery of Victoria along with a John Olsen. At first young painters came from everywhere. Painters are like that. If there is a place to show their work, they come like flies – that is, at the beginning of their careers. They also love galleries with money.

We put a large John Howley on the wall. As well, I tried to buy a smaller one and every week would give him a little bit of money from the takings until I paid it all off. I still have that painting – it is a fierce beast painted in bright colours. Lawrence Daws, Donald Laycock, Clifton Pugh and his wife Marlene came to the café. Yvette Anderson was a unique, beautiful young painter but she always invented stories, and being gullible, I would believe them all – swimmers in lakes in the middle of nowhere, waiting for a lover. She was like the character in *Le Grand Meaulnes*. Ethel Barnes, a painter of a certain age, would also come. Mervyn Cassidy, a friend of Erica McGilchrist, would come; both were very eloquent at CAS meetings. Mrs Vassilieff was a great orator, the best of all. Charles and Barbara Blackman. Roy Opie was very colourful. Harry Raynor, who later gave up painting for a bookshop. Ann Taylor, Edith Wall, Frank Werther. Mary Talbot was very decorative and good at giving fabulous parties. Peter Burns, of course, and many more young hopefuls, as well as Gino Nibbi Arthur Boyd, Edith Wall, Roma Ward, Ian Sime, Dawn Sime – it seems as many males as females. The CAS was an avant-garde movement, after all.

Roy Opie arrived once from Adelaide and he had a bleeding

finger. Blood fell everywhere in the café but he was jolly and welcome. There was also a mad man who came in regularly eating icecream and who walked in the streets of Melbourne amongst the cars. He had been the premier violinist at the Melbourne Symphony Orchestra. He was much loved and pitied and we often gave him a coffee. I think Tim Burstall used him in one of his films, *The Prize*. He also wanted my two boys and myself, but I refused, not wanting to endure the sad violinist on location with my boys. I didn't sleep for three nights until I came to that decision, as Tim Burstall was a young filmmaker and needed all the help he could get. I was sad to say no. Tim used his two sons instead, and maybe another mother.

My husband and I often worked together, but sometimes we would run the restaurant in turn, which allowed us to stay with our little children and me to attend to my work as well. Babysitters were scarce and would sometimes disappear with our children, causing us a terrible fright.

John and Sunday thought that once we'd opened the café we could leave our children with Joy Hester and Gray Smith in Belgrave and this would be a little income for Joy. Joy had Peregrine, who was Philippe's age, and Fern, who was younger than William. My heart was very heavy to be parted from my children. William was just starting to walk. We went every Sunday to see them and leave them. One night, when it was my turn to be at the Mirka Café, a taxi stopped outside about 10.30pm and Joy Hester in tears and out of her mind, holding a smiling William in her arms, had come all the way from Belgrave to bring me William who had eaten some Ratsak. He had found a packet on the floor. Joy had given him water and salt for vomiting but William kept drinking the water and not vomiting. We rang Dr Allan Wynn, who came promptly and took William to the Alfred Hospital and all was well eventually. We then took an Italian nana and both children came back home after that adventure.

One afternoon, as I was alone at the Mirka Café, a charming man and a beautiful woman came in the door, desperate to get a real French sandwich. It was Sir Robert Helpmann and Katharine Hepburn. I made a splendid ham in a baguette sandwich. Melvyn Douglas came to town for a play and discovered the Mirka Café. We became great friends and soon Melvyn Douglas spent his weekends with the Mora family and friends. One day we thought we could spend a weekend in Geelong and take Melvyn, to show him another aspect of Australia. He had with him a lovely young companion, so she came also. Klaus and Gertie Anschel, our first friends in Australia, came with their two children Miriam and Danny. As soon as we arrived at the hotel Melvyn Douglas figured out the place quickly. No tea or service after 8.00pm, no matter how I pleaded with the manager of the hotel, famous actor or not. Melvyn Douglas took a sleeping tablet and went to sleep promptly and we were left with his girl companion who had taken a happy tablet, so the only thing I could do was organise a game of hide-and-seek in the corridors of the hotel until our guest would feel tired and we could all go to sleep. The children had a lovely time out of this adventure in a hotel.

Johnny Cranko, ballet choreographer, was in town and was a delight; he walked into our studio hardly touching the ground and predicted great futures for my little children. Paula Hinton and Walter Gore from the Ballet Rambert were in town also. Walter wanted Charles Blackman and Joy Hester to design sets for his ballets and wanted some Shostakovich music, not to be found in Melbourne in 1955. Paula and Walter were great friends of Sally Gilmour (later Sally Wynn), the famous ballerina, who was a very rare artist and beautiful soul and person. So parties were endlessly organised from the café for our cherished weekends. Many were spent at Klaus and Gertie Anschel's, who had a big house and balcony in Kew, and at Sally and Allan Wynn's place, also a large house. David Wynn, Allan's brother, was a friend of Clifford Last and Julius Kane, and through them we met the Wynns.

Saturday mornings were always kept for breakfast with the Percevals. The café was a kind of home on these mornings – more facilities for cooking than in the studio and more food. All our cups and saucers were made by John Perceval and many were stolen, as they were works of art. So we kept giving more orders for more cups and saucers.

Cupid with his arrow went upstairs and downstairs and many romances started at the Mirka Café, and great dramas. Frank Werther was very worried about my attachment to one of the painters. Suffice to say that it was at the Mirka Café that Georges and I gave each other back our wedding rings. John Reed's prophecy?

Great excitement when we decided to have a show at the café of Joy Hester's great work. I can still feel the atmosphere of the café; all her works were black and white and some people called the Mirka Café a funeral parlour while the show was on. Yet the work was so vibrant and tumultuous, like Joy's mind. Just like a song of Edith Piaf's. The work tore you to pieces if you dared to look at it, particularly the little love drawings of Joy and Gray as lovers in bed. Only two works sold, one to Georges Mora and one to me. Eight pounds each, or eight guineas we used to say. All the same, our passion for art didn't diminish. On the contrary there was a battle to win there. One drawing by my son Philippe sold for ten shillings and was bought by the famous English literary critic, Lionel Trilling.

Every night people would come to the Mirka Café and sit on the stairs up to the first floor with their coffee and open sandwiches, as downstairs was packed. We played records in those days, endless French singers and also songs from the plays in town. 'I Talk To The Trees' was my favourite song, from *South Pacific*. One young ballet dancer, David McIllwraith, would be a faithful customer, his fame was not his dancing but his inheritance. But no one believed him. Eventually it was true and he was rich and we were all glad for him. He invested all his money in a cabaret, not far from the Mirka Café, and lost it all.

For two of my true coffee drinkers I would make a coffee *à la main*; that is, in a little saucepan, the French way. Boil the water, throw the ground coffee in the boiling water, put the lid on, don't let it boil again, just sit a little on the fire. One coffee drinker was Alex Jelinek, who was a brilliant architect but due to laws was not allowed to build as he had studied overseas and not here. We were sad but he still did build sometimes. He wanted to build a studio entirely made of glass for me in Shakespeare Grove in Hawthorn, and to have privacy, at the press of a button steam would come and fill the space between two big sheets of glass that formed the walls. But in 1955 we were not allowed to build it. The other charming coffee drinker was Dr James Durham, the future father of the painter Kate Durham. He loved the Mirka Café and the 9 Collins Street studio. My husband and myself, we adored him. In those days, we had endless conversations about the nuclear fallout. We were haunted by it.

One summer afternoon, hardly anyone in the café but James Durham and myself. He wore a beautiful light suit and, lo and behold, dropped his cup of coffee sitting at the bar, all over the magnificent suit. He left promptly without a word and came back a little while later, wearing a new suit. I was quite puzzled by this turn of events. James Durham was the partner of Dr Ainslie Meares, two different kinds of men. John Reed once asked Ainslie Meares to open one of my exhibitions but he refused and never came to our studio. Often patients would have a session with Ainslie Meares in Spring Street and then come to my studio; often they were sad and I would cheer them up. Maybe that is why A. Meares refused to open my exhibition. John Reed was quite flummoxed by A. Meares' reaction to me.

We had a beautiful large bain-marie in the café and I often thought it was like the entrails of a big boat. I loved the bain-marie, a comforting large kind of stove keeping my *blanquette de veau* warm, and my *boeuf bourguignon* delicious. One man, Bob Cugley, who printed the CAS invitations and often books no one else wanted to print, including the journal *Angry Penguins*, would come very often from his Bourke Street printing place to stare at me and mostly to eat my boeuf bourguignon that he kept calling goulash – this annoyed me but I never told him. It was his way of teasing me. As a young man in 1911, he'd worked at the National Press, and worked on the printing of the great book, *Australia Unlimited*, of which I am a proud owner. Later, Bob Cugley became the owner of the National Press. His great story was to have been invited by Sidney Myer to come and join him in his endeavours – to have been chosen and say no. Bob wanted to do it alone, but he was very proud of this encounter with the famous Sidney Myer.

Bob had many tales to tell and had a fierce judgement of people and politics. Once he was very honoured when a male journalist-cum-gangster, who was always in and out of jail, left all his manuscripts to Bob when he died. I have forgotten the name of this wild man. He would be invited to all the best houses over the weekend and then tell all the next Monday in the papers. Mostly Portsea and Sorrento houses. Bob loved my drawings and would always make sure I had reams of cartridge paper in my studio. He printed the first book of poems by Geoffrey Dutton and *The Vegetative Eye* by Max Harris.

He would also tell me which prime minister was good or bad, and thus I learnt a bit more about politics in Australia. Bob was much loved by many interesting people in Melbourne. When later I started my life alone, Bob would take me once a month for lunch at Florentino. He would say, 'I never believed I would take out a grandma for lunch.' He would invite fabulous guests as well to share our lunch. Eric Thake, a printer and artist, and John Reed once. The writer Stephen Murray-Smith and his wife. Bob was pleased when in 1980 I took a photo of him on which to base one of the tutors' masks I made for the play *Medea*.

One day I developed a very bad sore on my left calf, the sore would not go away. My long skirts would get dusty going down the stairs to the kitchen and up again a thousand times, carrying basketfuls of empty cups. Dr Denton, who was an *habitué* also, took care of my sore and cured it, leaving a very pretty little round scar on my leg to remember it. I was most grateful to Dr Denton, whose wife Dame Margot was also a great friend of Sally Wynn.

Norma Miller came to town with her band and became great friends with John Howley, who is also a fine musician as well as a painter. Norma Miller opened the show at the Victorian Society Gallery of the four painters Cliff Pugh, Donald Laycock, Lawrence Daws and John Howley. A great event at the time in the art world, as their work sold, a rare thing in those days. They were the brilliant students from the National Gallery of Victoria art school. But it was Janet Dawson who won a grant to go overseas to further her studies. Janet and I loved Lorenzo Lotto, the Italian painter, early sixteenth century. I had the Bernard Berenson book, *Lorenzo Lotto*, and she coveted it.

Neil Douglas, the potter and poet and painter, friend of the Percevals and John and Sunday, would come to the Mirka Café. He was an earthman personified; when you saw him you would feel the love of the country, the same as Aboriginal people make you feel, that love of the land and its mysteries.

It was very hard working at the Mirka Café as it became the toast of Melbourne, and, because many interesting people came, one had to engage with writers, painters, musicians, actors, photographers, journalists and teenagers. But outside, the world was a dangerous place: we were not allowed to keep a beautiful black cat in the café, he had to go. I was heartbroken.

Somehow the restaurant café we had was getting too small and not comfortable enough to run, and also took too much time away from my painting. And we had no licence to serve and enjoy wine. Everything has to grow, expand, be better, so we soon had to say goodbye to *la vie de bohème* in Exhibition Street and open a real restaurant in Wellington Street, East Melbourne – after a year of preparation where Charles Blackman was a cook with Georges. In 1958 the Balzac was born and what a restaurant it was, run impeccably by Georges Mora. *Le tout* Melbourne came. I thought we could have angel *appliqués* on the walls and we asked John Perceval to make them, and this commission started John on his famous angels series. There was a little angel in a tree we couldn't quite put on the wall and Sunday snatched it from me. I was very upset. Georges would have given it to her perhaps. It is now in the National Gallery of Victoria but mine still in my heart.

Rosemary Ryan, a painter and a friend, thought copper leaves on the ceiling would be beautiful and we agreed. Georges decided on the banquettes, the tables, the chairs; chose pretty waitresses, a French wine waiter, a chef and second chef and good French dishes, and we were away into the sixties.

I sewed the tablecloths and serviettes with my beloved Singer machine and sometimes a new lot was done that very morning to be used the same night, if the laundry didn't deliver in time. David Boyd got the commission to make wine carafes. Very handsome they were. Winifred Atwell launched the Balzac with the then French consul and Ken Brodziak.

Balzac was the first restaurant to receive a 10pm alcohol licence. Mr Rylah, the chief of police, would sometimes have wine in his glass after 10pm and then leave a little later. As soon as he left, the police would come to investigate to see if alcohol was served after 10pm. It was really a Ned Kelly story. (The Nolan paintings at Heide had made the Kelly story familiar to us and my little boys.)

Charles Munch, the great French conductor, came and his aura and charm was magic. When he called me *ma chérie* as I gave him a drawing – a large pen and ink one – I was a goner, but I stayed in Melbourne. He loved all my work in charcoal, pen and ink which decorated the walls upstairs. Stanley Kramer came to Melbourne for his film *On the Beach*, and would come for dinner almost every night and continue to work over dinner with his crew and actors – Anthony Perkins was most charming. Stanley Kramer was like a bomb about to explode. One night, when all the customers had left, he had a terrible vocal fight with his wife. The scene was late at night, Mrs Kramer was upstairs on the landing and Stanley Kramer was downstairs as they harangued each other. I always sat next to him, it seemed to calm him down. I remember him saying that until the age of forty-five years he would walk in New York with not a dime in his pocket but films in his head, and then success started.

Sabrina and her mother would sit pretty for lunch. She did have these breasts and the tiniest waist ever. Marlene Dietrich also had a chaperone; she always ordered the best wine, red usually, and made sure we kept the wine left in the bottle for her lunch next day: always a tiny piece of red meat and salad. Usually one would leave the wine for the chef if some was left in the bottle.

One day, Georges was overseas and I had just come back from Aspendale with the children when the Balzac rang to say that Maurice Chevalier had arrived for lunch. Well, I organised the children and went to the Balzac to meet Maurice Chevalier, whose legend I had grown up with – he had enormous warmth and he liked the Balzac and me very much. He stayed at the Windsor Hotel and I would meet him in the Fitzroy Gardens, pushing my big pram with Tiriel in it. M. Chevalier loved a large painting I had in the *Herald* Art Show at the time and understood my soul. I have a picture of Maurice Chevalier and me, he insisted that we be photographed with the painting. We had long conversations about one's dedication to one's art and at one grand lunch at Balzac I was sitting on his left.

Maurice Chevalier: 'Mirka, I will ask you a question, it might not happen, but if it did happen, I would like to know what you would do – could you choose between your family or your art?'

Mirka: 'I would choose my art.'

Maurice Chevalier: 'This is what I wanted to hear.' And the party went on and I was not the same.

I think the success of the Balzac was that Georges was a perfect host and was there lunch and dinner without fail. Sometimes I would get a call from Georges when I was at home; if Georges could not remember a name, he would describe the person, the table, what the person ate, and I would remember the name. Once a year, Georges would travel for a holiday and I would take over the running of the restaurant, that is why I knew the names of most customers as they became *habitués*. Actors would often come in a hurry before their *entrée en scène*. Graham Kennedy, young and nervous and in a hurry before his show, came to eat almost every night. I can still see his slim silhouette. One night Charles Reddington, an American painter in Melbourne, came to the Balzac after his opening at South Yarra Gallery with Asher Bilu and Bob Hughes. Bob in those days was *très chou chou*, very pretty – *la coqueluche de ces dames sûrement*. He would come at other times and sit alone at a little table, writing his *Art of Australia*.

Balzac was a *défilé* of the best, the most talented, the most wicked of Melbourne; it was a cultured island in a city that was still very square, conservative. Mrs Cairns I always loved and understood and could feel her devotion to Jim Cairns. I remember the entrance one night of the great hostess Mrs Sheila Wood, famous not only for her parties but for the roses at Flemington on Melbourne Cup Day, and her husband Sam, young, handsome, and both dressed beautifully. We became great friends and their parties at home were a real work of art, with a mixture of fine people for good conversation and power, if you liked such things.

I was very often hungry at the Balzac because I didn't like to eat in public or I didn't like the waitresses serving me. But when I would think of oysters I would lose all my notions of *égalité*. I would write in my little notebooks, sitting at the desk, trying to describe the atmosphere, the waitresses, *the va-et-vient* of various bottles of wine disappearing in glasses. The way men held their cigarettes, the couples who didn't speak to each other right through their meals. This was very curious to me.

A little extract from my little notebook, 29th June 1962: '*Je trouve écrire très difficile; pour entrer au fond des choses il faut complètement s'en séparer.*' 'I find writing extremely difficult; to go deeply into a subject you have to separate yourself from it.'

When Georges became ill in 1964, I had to go every day to Balzac and could not have my quota of drawing and studies; I didn't like my new life but had to wait until Georges' recovery. During those days I experienced a recurring dream: I was a little girl and I was playing in the middle of the street, rather a road, particularly *ensoleillée*, and in the middle of the road was a lovely white bed with white-bluish sheets, white blankets. Everything was white and I could not see the construction of the bed. One felt only a soft and cosy bed and in that bed full of sunlight a beautiful black wolf was lying down on his back and I was taking care of him, covering him with a blanket. He seemed very docile, same as one plays with a doll. I realised that I had not painted for two weeks, so the dream had rather an intriguing palette and kept me busy in my daydreaming. Sometimes I was very sleepy but didn't know I was. I would then draw little pen and ink *esquisses* and wake up.

The big wonder at Balzac for me was which waitresses went to bed with which customer; all was very discreet, but if I watched carefully I could see which waitress was blushing while serving a certain table. It was one of the waitresses who taught me how to use a Dutch cap. I had had no knowledge of these things before. My doctor had not told me, but when I asked him he wrote a prescription for the size of the cap. He didn't tell me about the KY jelly so I was in big trouble for a while, until I spoke to the same waitress, who gave me yet another lesson in the use of the cap. I was most grateful to be less ignorant in these matters.

Some nights at Balzac were fabulous, just like the parties we had at 9 Collins Street. When Perceval and his wife Mary came we would draw with *mousse au chocolat* and ashes of cigarettes, and pen sometimes. When all the customers had left we would go into the kitchen and rampage the food, and we had great uninterrupted conversations that way, until the early hours of the morning. When Bert Tucker returned from overseas, we gave him a big party full of painters at the Balzac – every guest brought a bag of birdseed as Bert was painting his Australian native birds. Seeds were every-where. I just remember the long table and noisy hum of voices and a lot of teasing.

In the meantime Georges got well again and took the restau-rant well in hand, until one of the waitresses started to buy paintings at Violet Dulieu's gallery, and she also had a very expen-sive wedding party at the Southern Cross. Once, she bought an expensive Blackman painting and we could not understand how she could afford it. Georges found out: the money came from the restaurant's takings. The painting was returned to the gallery and the money to the restaurant.

The police were after bribes and Georges always refused to give bribes. For many nights when the Balzac closed, the police cars would chase Georges' car all the way through Wellington Street to 9 Collins Street. It was very unpleasant. The bribes were for being allowed to serve wine later than 10pm, but we always stopped at 10pm. Having lived through a war it was peculiar to have this kind of behaviour to deal with in Melbourne.

Nights at the Balzac with the theatre critic Geoffrey Hutton and his lovely wife. Both writers. Charles Bush and Phyl Waterhouse –

painters. Helen Homewood, always majestic, and Laurie Simpson, a faithful friend. John Kirkbride – an *habitué*. John Dobell (no relation to William), who lived at Cliveden Mansions nearby. Mr and Mrs Violet Dulieu. I remember Mr Dulieu being French and having one of the best cellars in town. A white wine, *Côte d'Or* especially. It always intrigued me how people find their way to the same place on the same night, at the same time, not knowing each other. Maybe it is the first hot north wind of springtime that is the cause. I think the Balzac was a magnet, a place at which to be seen and to drink in the atmosphere. Time for new flowers. Georges always loved flowers on the dining tables; he would go with his scissors for a little walk and cut flowers that were calling him, coming out of pretty fences in East Melbourne.

Art history excerpt: one day a well-known London gallery owner came to Balzac for lunch and stayed all day, all painters at attention. He especially loved Charles Blackman's work, and many others of course. John Perceval prepared me a canvas nailed onto a board so I could do some work and show it to the gallery owner when he came to my studio; he loved my work. We were filmed for the newsreels on either side of the painting and I was glad to be part of the show as it was an historic event – Australian painters in London. One night at Balzac – one of the great nights, when prospects grow and wine is drunk – a young gallery director from New Zealand came and was staying in our studio in Collins Street for the night. The gallery owner took a great liking to this young man and when it was time to close the Balzac, Georges, myself and the young man took our London visitor to his hotel. As we got out of the taxi, the young man said to me, 'Mirka, hang on to me.' In no time the gallery owner was pulling one arm of the young New Zealander, and I the other, and the gallery owner had to go to his hotel without his desire fulfilled. Next day I was crossed off the list of exhibitors for the London show and was very sad.

The Balzac was indeed a dangerous place for career making for painters. I wonder what was happening to the careers and marriages of writers, psychiatrists and others at the time. But fun was in the air and great excitement. Lady Casey, a great art patron and very talented herself, would come with her friend Frances Burke and Phoebe, Frances's partner. Lady Casey wrote a beautiful book of poems and often described to me her childhood in Collins Street when you could still see a lovely garden behind her father's consulting room. Once, when I was walking alone in the Fitzroy Gardens, a bit forlorn, Lady Casey, walking towards me, said, 'What is the matter, Mirka, are you sad?'

'I have a big problem,' I said, 'too much dust in my studio.'

Lady Casey said, 'Do not worry, dust is nourishing.' So I felt better with that profound remark.

Rudy Komon, a Sydney art dealer, came one day and made his deal with Len French. Len was very aware of a new departure and told me how important his meeting had been at Balzac with Rudy Komon. Another time Rudy Komon came with William Dobell for lunch, a long lunch. Everyone had gone and William Dobell was sitting on the banquette next to me, opposite Rudy Komon who was staring at us. William Dobell did a great portrait of me on the tablecloth, I promptly went to the kitchen to get a big knife to cut the portrait out of the tablecloth. We all looked at it, very pleased, and when it was time to go, Rudy Komon took the portrait and was about to fold it and put it in his pocket, when Dobell said, 'No, this is for Mirka.' I was very honoured.

That same night William Dobell had a show at the Museum of Modern Art in Tavistock Place. I came disguised as a schoolgirl, borrowing a uniform from Miriam Anschel – Klaus and Gertie's daughter – and looking like a Charles Blackman painting. The taxi outside the house waited as I transformed myself, and when I came back the taxi driver didn't recognise me and wouldn't let me in the cab, thinking I was a young child. Eventually I told him I was the same person who had come out of his cab earlier. William Dobell recognised me straight away, but many people at the exhibition were not sure and some said, 'Excuse me, are you Mirka Mora?' Sometimes I said yes, sometimes I said no.

Sir Thomas Playford, the Premier of South Australia, loved to draw at the Balzac. Marcel Marceau at the Balzac with John, Sunday, Georges and I under the beautiful Perceval angels on the walls. All is perfect and it is 1963 and I managed to have a show of charcoal drawings in Brisbane and praise from Gertrude Langer, the critic. I almost forgot to come back home but Georges was due for his yearly trip overseas and I had to go back to Melbourne to run the Balzac, which was our dream, and which had become a goldmine and perpetual party, where at last people paid for their dinners – except some painters and poets didn't (the tradition of a good restaurant). Max Harris and his wife Yvonne loved the Balzac and understood Georges' style and aims and admired him very much.

Senator Reginald 'Spot' Turnbull and his wife Elizabeth, great friends of John Reed's, would come often to Balzac and always caused a commotion. The trouble was that Mr Turnbull was upstairs with a mistress and Mrs Turnbull was downstairs with someone else. The great art of the Balzac restaurant was to make sure both couples would not meet. The bills were organised in such a way that they were not given at the same time, to allow the couple downstairs to leave before the couple upstairs. It required great subtlety from the chef, waitresses and wine waiters to organise it all – it always worked. This was Balzac turning into a theatre with live comedy and drama. A very French restaurant.

Elizabeth Turnbull was adamant that I needed a blind date. I didn't know what a blind date meant. She organised it in Canberra and I missed out terribly on a most desirable, charming writer. As he took me to my hotel, after exchanging a book for a drawing in his studio, I by mistake said goodbye to another car on the step of the hotel, one that looked like the car of my ex-lover. So my blind date must have thought me peculiar not waving to him but to someone else. He tried many successive years to catch me, but to no avail.

Soon, in 1965, Balzac Restaurant had to be sold as the Paris end of Collins Street was to be demolished and we had to look for another home. This time we wanted to have an art gallery, a restaurant, a studio for me and a house for the family, all at once. A gallery because the Museum of Modern Art was in recess. The restaurant to entertain our friends, studio for my work, and home for the Mora family and cats. So one day Georges announced to me that he had bought the Tolarno Hotel and that I should surely be happy as I would have a large studio this time – after looking at many houses without studios. It was lovely to have so much space and to explore all the rooms. I made some research on the history of Tolarno, but it was hard to get material until the day Judith Wright, the poet, came for dinner after her husband had died a while before. I had met the poet through Barbara and Charles Blackman. She knew a lot about Tolarno as her late husband had been a jackeroo in his youth at the Tolarno station in Victoria, and Tolarno in Fitzroy Street had been home once. Where our new restaurant was to be, had been a garden where people played croquet. In that remarkable book *Australia Unlimited* there is a picture of Tolarno station with all the farmhands and their bicycles, quite a poetic picture.

Slowly more people came and told us story after story. One very old man, called Mr Twentyman, had been a lodger for many years in the hotel and his fame was that his grandmother or mother had danced with Ned Kelly as a young man – everybody loved Ned Kelly in the country. The blacksmiths would shoe the horses back to front so when Ned Kelly rode one way the horseshoe went the other way and would mislead the policemen. With all the paintings by Sidney Nolan at Heide, we were well versed in Ned Kelly stories, but this one was the best.

Tolarno was the first hotel who had electric bells to call the maids and butlers. You could still see them in some large rooms. Mostly near the mantelpieces above the fireplaces. Also at the Tolarno, Mr Sidney Myer parted from his first wife – endless stories came about and fed my imagination as I love the Victorian era in Melbourne. The growth of a city and its people.

There was much to be done in that restaurant – it needed a new kitchen and new toilets. Soon the main large dining room, which was to have been my studio, was to be the art gallery and I was given the bridal room, which was very splendid. The boys had their own rooms and a new life emerged with two cats, Napoléon and Stiffy, who always sat on the desk and growled at people or scratched people as they came to pay their bills. We all lived on the first floor of the hotel. The hotel was much bother to Georges and me as we were not really experienced. We had a manager, but this did not work either; people would make terrible noise at night and Georges would go out in his dressing gown trying to quieten them, with me following Georges as I was frightened for him.

Eventually, we had to sell the hotel, which meant Georges

could concentrate on the restaurant and gallery. I also lost my great studio and descended right to the cellars where my studio turned into three rooms, and many of our goods occupied other rooms. The cellar smelled like a Bendigo mine, two hundred metres down in the earth, but I loved it. The light came from windows flush to the footpath so I watched many legs of all kinds passing by. One day a fire started, one day it was burgled, but life went on – one day it was flooded also. All the Mora bedrooms shifted downstairs and yet another era started with fabulous exhibitions that Georges organised while in Paris: Renoir, Lautrec, Picasso, Chagall, and also excellent Australian artists. Many customers who were originally from the Mirka Café went to Balzac to be engaged, came to Tolarno as married people with children. The restaurant was again the toast of Melbourne, even though some people said it would not work as in those days Fitzroy Street had a very bad reputation, with drugs, prostitution, Squizzy Taylor legends. It seems that, as usual, Georges was ahead of his time. Many parties would follow great openings, and again I was watching the secret life of the waitresses, the chef, the wine waiter, and again, when Georges went away every year, I would take over.

Once, the wine waiter wanted to leave and promised Georges that he would wait for his return, but naturally the wine waiter left as soon as Georges went and there I was with the job of finding a wine waiter. I advertised the position and many applicants came with fabulous CVs. Some were tall, some were thin, some were little, all with very good qualities. After three sleepless nights (I always need three nights to solve problems) and three horrendous days, I still could not choose and more excellent applicants kept coming. I finally decided to forget all the attributes a wine waiter should have and just choose a man I would like to go to bed with.

Just an idea for a choice, so one day a beautiful Irish man came, speaking beautiful English, well dressed, attractive, not old, not young. He appealed to me and so he was my choice, and was impeccable in his work, but what he did not tell me was that he had a wife and seven children and a very attractive mistress, and this would cause from time to time some drama. When Georges returned he approved of my choice but I didn't tell him the motives behind my choice. Suffice to say that I had no intention of going to bed with the wine waiter, it had just been a dream – or lateral thinking.

Soon I wanted to paint all the walls, like good painters do when they see walls. Martin Sharp came down from Sydney and helped me paint leaves and roses on doors and windows of the restaurant. Nugget Coombs was a regular diner but as the years passed he preferred fresh fruits to eat, as opposed to normal meals. Bill Snedden loved the scallops cooked *à la minute* and came often. His great story, which he loved to tell and had everyone roaring with laughter, was how when making love he would fall out of bed so often. Don Chipp was *assidu* also and very excitable. Once a charming man came and looked at me and asked if I was born in Romania. 'No,' I said, 'but my mother and grandparents were.' It was the great conductor Zubin Mehta. Elections came and elections went; late into the night Mrs A. Peacock dancing on the table and making speeches while Andrew sat patiently and I wanted to close the café and go to sleep.

One night, Charles Blackman and Thelma Clune – the wife of the writer Frank Clune – a few other people and myself started to break some of the wooden chairs in the front restaurant room after midnight, a dangerous time. Mr Mora, as I used to call my husband, waited until the effervescent breaking stopped and next day ordered more chairs. He was the perfect host. There was in Paris a restaurant of long ago where if the diner refused to go out through the door but wanted to leave through one of the walls, the host would have the bricks taken out and then the customer could go out through the large hole in the wall. It was a very famous Russian restaurant where I went as a young bride. When my son William went to Paris to pick up some artwork, Mr Brassai, whose work it was, took William to this famous place. Mrs Brassai, who didn't go, was not pleased with her husband for taking a young man to this notorious restaurant. This restaurant reminds me of Sir John Longstaff, who had to paint General Monash's white horse. The horse refused to get into the studio through the main door. Sir John Longstaff had to take bricks out of the studio at the back and the horse agreed to come in.

It was at Tolarno that we saw the moon being visited by earthlings and life was never quite the same after it. I wore astronaut suits and was teased. The Blackmans came back from France and stayed in the hotel upstairs. Barry Humphries and his first wife Rosalind and daughters Tessa and Emily came to see Charles and Barbara. My son Philippe thought at his tender teen age that all artists go on leaving, everyone has to cope, to survive, otherwise you are left behind. He also thought artists have something akin in their manner of speaking.

An elegant diner and his girlfriend would book a room upstairs after a meal to celebrate and he was a well-known married man – but *noblesse oblige*. We were all very envious and discreet and full of wonder at such style of dining and afternoon nap.

One Sunday, late morning, a dead girl in Room 34 was discovered. The night before, she was saying good night to all of us at the desk and asking especially not to be woken up too early. How sad – a case of abortion, the police said.

The chef at Balzac was an English man and a very strong Catholic with many children to feed. When his wife could not produce children any more the marriage fell apart and I was very puzzled. I saw him once in Hobart and once in Canberra, both times crossing a street. Me going one way, he going the other way – such is life. Charles came back from Sydney where he went with Georges, both well dressed; Charles had a dark suit and looked like a doll. Elwyn Lynn told Charles that he was watching me, for one day I was going to come out with something big. How clever he was! Elwyn Lynn wrote books on art and was a painter and art critic who loved 9 Collins Street. Al Alvarez, the writer of *The Savage God*, the book on suicide, was always tempting Charles with 'birds', Charles tells me. Charles talking about his trip in Holland, Ostend, Vienna. Arthur Boyd always opening windows, Charles always shutting them.

Soon Tolarno had two galleries, one in front and one at the back. We showed the Sidney Nolan paintings of Ned Kelly and it was a great event and a great catalogue. John, Sunday and Georges hung the show in the front gallery on the same walls I was to have. The director Josef von Sternberg opened my show and the Film Festival on the same night. Sternberg was a most delicious 73-year-old man. *Hélas*, he thought he was too old, he had sold all his art collections of great masters and his sculptures. I asked him what he liked to do best now. Well, I got a surprise, and it was not what you might think. His great pleasure was to go in his garden in LA and, holding a torch, a fire one, he liked to burn the spiders.

The Great American Art Show came to Melbourne, and the director of the National Gallery in London came to Tolarno and promptly was besotted with one of our waitresses, who preferred girls. We had organised a great dinner in the back room, where the walls were covered with great paintings and the atmosphere was electric. Josef von Sternberg early on decided to ask for his coat. It was a kind of duffle coat, slightly military. I was curious why he put his coat on an hour before leaving; he said he wanted to shake hands with all the people in the front room, and because he wore his coat people would know that he was leaving. I was so impressed to see that great film director still working in normal life ceremoniously.

Adrian Lawlor came one lunchtime with the art patron and writer Margaret Carnegie. The book *Arquebus* that Adrian Lawlor wrote in 1937 John Reed had made me read earlier on. Adrian and I exchanged addresses but he died a little while later. I have his face printed in my mind forever. He evoked his fantastic book, *Arquebus*. And I remember people in size and fame larger than life coming for lunch and dinner. Clyde Packer and Bert Newton, creating a party atmosphere that never ended. Sir Charles Spry, chief of ASIO, got to like me very much and when he heard I was coming to Canberra he organised a car and chauffeur to take me to the War Memorial. My friends, Dr and Mrs Tom Smyth, escorted me and we had great excitement chasing another car just for fun, in very quiet Canberra. Sir Charles Spry would have long talks to me about him being firm and not taking the hand of dying young soldiers calling their mothers. Sir Charles said, 'You have to die like a man.' He did not take the hand of the dying boys as he passed by them in the field of war, and he thought my seventeen-year-old son Philippe's drawings were cruel!

The ASIO men also came to Tolarno. They were large men in black suits and unreal in their powerful presence – a bit like Buster Keaton, Laurel and Hardy, or The Three Stooges. But we all kept a straight face. The Vietnam War came in the midst of it all, causing havoc to families, with fathers wanting their sons to go to war and mothers not exactly keen. Glen Tomasetti wrote plays about it and at Tolarno we would talk about the families in turmoil and what to do. The Honourable Jean McLean went to jail fighting against sending young boys to war. There were other brilliant women, and men. Annie Gillison and Mary Craig (now Noor) were journalists with the *Age*. Anne Boyd was a composer; Stephanie Bennett, Jill Gray and Jenny Ham were PR women. Tony Morphett was a writer and filmmaker, and Anne Pickburn was an ABC interviewer. A cavalcade of brilliant people making the Tolarno a titanic restaurant with their vibrancy, and catastrophes happening to almost everyone.

One night Charles Blackman and I were guarding the Tolarno while Georges was overseas and we got bored. I got a very wicked idea to amuse ourselves. I was wearing a black velvet top and my idea was to cut a little hole where my nipples were and let them out and watch the customers as they came to pay their bills. Charles and I kept a straight face. Most people pretended not to see what they were seeing; some really looked, and eventually Charles and I could make great observations on the way people reacted and we burst into laughter as soon as they left. It was not a boring evening any more.

Another night, as I was again running the Tolarno, the chef had a quarrel with the waitress who was his mistress, and both left. The place was packed but we managed to survive the night. Once, George Baldessin threw black coffee on a lady's fur collar and caused havoc in the restaurant. The lady's table of five other guests were from the country. They were wild with fury. I offered to pay the dry-cleaning bill for the coat, I offered not to charge them for their dinner. For Baldessin, it was really performance art. He was sitting with a table of painters and they were amused. I was not quite amused. Dame Peggy van Praagh, then the Director of the Australian Ballet, who was dining there that night, sided with the country people and this confused me no end. She was my friend, after all, and she knew that artists went overboard sometimes.

I miss the restaurant life; one could feel the tempo of the city, meet brilliant journalists whose writing you admired. My knowledge of great Australian wines was a real schoolbook of vineyards and localities, geography. But my favourite wine, and I kept many bottles of it under the bed, was Château d'Yquem dessert wine. I drank many bottles of this. Faces without names remain in my mind and many names without a face remain in my memories. The *va-et-vient*. The booking of tables. The menus. The seasons. The people from overseas. I still have many Balzac dockets signed but never paid. But I cherish them. The waiters and waitresses. The hum of the kitchen noises. The intrigues great and small. The gossip and how young we all were. The fashions. Once a young photographer said to me about my clothes, 'Mirka, you are so far out that you are in.' Lovely Jean Shrimpton dined often before the Melbourne Cup where she caused such a sensation wearing a little skirt above the knee. Andrés Segovia, the great Spanish guitarist, came for lunch with his beautiful secretary and could only think of a siesta with his young assistant. His magic fingers were like sausages and you wondered how he could be such a great musician. The muscles in his fingers told the story.

Many people disappeared into the future and sank in no-land time, a few survived and shone like stars in the Australian sky. Big stars. Like Pompeii, the last days of Tolarno were coming close. One night, early in 1970, I came home at about midnight, and as I passed my husband's room, the door opened and a beautiful girl came out. I kept walking to my room, which was next in the long corridor, and entered my bedroom and pondered what I had just seen. *Le coeur gros*. I didn't think she'd come to sing him a lullaby.

Next morning, my husband said that I had to leave. I was dumbfounded but I never argued with my husband so I decided to leave. But I asked my husband, via my son William, to go to Sydney as I didn't want him to see me packing and leaving.

And so I left, starting my life alone in a house in Wellington Street, around the corner from Tolarno so I would not be far from the children. Georges insisted that the children stay with him, and even then I obeyed him. Maurice Chevalier's prophecy came true this time and I was very sad but brave. Soon Tolarno was sold to the restauranteur Leon Massoni and his wife, and my husband could fulfil his dream of having a gallery without a restaurant and concentrate on art. In the early 1980s he was awarded the Chevalier des Arts et des Lettres, a great honour in France. He died soon after, at the age of seventy-nine, just like John Reed, leaving a little boy from a second marriage aged seven.

LEFT (L to R) My maternal grandfather
(Myer Gelbein), Aunty Mimi and my
maternal grandmother (Mirka Gelbein),
Romania, circa 1920

RIGHT My mother with her brother in
Rotterdam, circa 1924

ABOVE LEFT My father in Paris

ABOVE RIGHT Paulette in the Luxembourg
Gardens, Paris, circa 1932

OPPOSITE, CLOCKWISE FROM TOP LEFT At
l'Ile-Adam, outside Paris, 1934; With Nouzette
at Saint-Malo, 1934; Holding my stomach in at
Deauville, 1936; Me at the age of two, very cross
with the photographer, Paris, 1930

ABOVE (L to R) My mother, me, Madame Rosa, Aunty Mimi, on the River Marne, outside Paris, circa 1937

LEFT School photo of (L to R) Marcelle, me, Salomèe, Paris, 1939

OPPOSITE TOP Georges (standing third from left, the only one wearing a tie) in the Foreign Legion, North Africa, 1941

OPPOSITE BOTTOM Georges at the Oeuvre de Secours aux Enfants orphanage, Hyere, 1942

OPPOSITE TOP Discussing the future
with Georges at Saint-Quay-Portrieux,
1946

OPPOSITE LEFT Doing a cartwheel
at Saint-Aygulf, 1950

OPPOSITE RIGHT Working at the
Oeuvre de Secours aux Enfants
orphanage, Saint-Quay-Portrieux,
1946. I decorated the truck and put
angels' wings on the children

RIGHT In the River le Doubs,
Pyrénées, 1950

ABOVE The painting in Paulette's apartment. I found this print in 1987 in Sydney's Paddington Market and paid $15 for it. I would have paid anything – it was my childhood. Number 9 Collins Street had the same feel as the studio in this painting

LEFT Paulette in her apartment in Paris. On the wall is the painting that so fascinated me as a child

OPPOSITE Georges and me in our wedding clothes, several weeks after our wedding, Paris, 1947

ABOVE Promenading with Georges and
Philippe, who is three months old, near Gare
Saint-Lazare, Paris, 1949

OPPOSITE Philippe and me at 9 Collins Street,
1954. The top and bottom paintings are by me,
the one in the middle is by Laurence Hope

ABOVE With actors and actresses at the opening
of the Mirka Café, 1954. Jean Sablon has just
smashed the champagne bottle; Allan Wynn is
behind me, to my left; and Athol Shmith's wife
Bambi is holding the cat in the window

TOP My mother as a farmer's wife in
Colchester, Connecticut, 1952

ABOVE LEFT Salomèe in her hospital bed,
Paris, 1946

ABOVE RIGHT The photo Harry Youlden
took by chance of Salomèe in Paris, 1960.
She was sitting in the flea market, where
my father had a shop

ABOVE The opening of the Balzac, 1958.
(L to R) Winifred Atwell; the French Consul,
Monsieur Lebas; Georges

BELOW With Sir Ralph Richardson, who opened
an exhibition by the Contemporary Art Society in
1954. The painting is by Laurence Hope

TOP Christmas at Aspendale, 1959. (L to R,
back) Sunday Reed, Georges; (front) Charles
Blackman, John Reed

BOTTOM (L to R) Charles Blackman, Barbara
Blackman, Sunday Reed, Aspendale, 1959

Pêle-Mêle: a Medley

oudouck was my father's favourite daughter. Her name was Salomèe and Doudouck was his tender name for her. As a little toddler, she developed diphtheria and my father carried her in his arms to take her to a hospital in Paris. She was light as a feather, my father kept telling us right through our childhood. As she grew up her *colonne vertébrale* was curving into an S, giving her one shoulder higher than the other – a lack of calcium.

Poor Salomèe had to wear corsets made of iron and leather and go to various sanatoriums. One was at La Rochelle en Charente on the Atlantic Ocean. I remember visiting her there with my mother. We went in a little boat to visit Oléron Island. One room in our apartment on rue Maître Albert contained all the corsets she grew out of. It was a sinister room. She was twelve when the Germans invaded France and we had to hide; we could not take her to a doctor, this caused her *colonne vertébrale* to develop into a real scoliosis.

As a child, my sister Salomèe never complained; she wanted to be a lettuce when she grew up and wanted to go to India. Later, she wrote poetry and was a painter right away. After the war, when she was eighteen, my father insisted that she be operated on by one of the best surgeons in Paris. My mother was against the operation. In those days, part of the tibia from one leg was grafted onto the first curve, and part of the other tibia was grafted onto the second curve. It was a terrible operation.

My sister stayed for one year in a bed of plaster. Eventually she could walk but her mind seemed to have gone amok: she remained in hospital all her life, outings were rare. When she seemed calmer, my father would take her home for a few days and she would write to me to say how happy she was to be home, but she would escape and scream in the street and was arrested every time. My poor father would take her back to the hospital from the police station. My father had remarried but he divorced his second wife, Fifine, to take care of his daughter Salomèe, as his wife could not cope.

My father, getting older, made his daughter a ward of the state. My youngest sister Marcelle used to go with her husband Roger to see Salomèe every year from Connecticut, USA, where she lived with her family, with my mother nearby. My mother said that I was not to go and see my sister Salomèe, she didn't go herself. Very odd statements and action. It is a terrible story and not a day passes without my thoughts flying to Salomèe. I write letters but she does not write any more; my letters are never replied to.

In January 1998 my sister Marcelle sent me a letter a doctor had kindly written to inform her that Salomèe was well and could leave the hospital, where she was in a room with 'difficult' patients.

The doctor's letter was two years old – my sister Marcelle does not write to me very often these days. As soon as I can I do want to see my sister, but I fear another breakdown as I would have to leave her in France because my home is in Australia. I hear my mother say I must not go. Strange. My mother knew me better than I knew myself, then, when she was alive. Marcelle worked for many years with geriatric people in a hospital. My father once told Marcelle's husband Roger that she was more intelligent than I am, and Roger told me what my father had said.

Poor Roger shot himself in the early 1990s. He was unable to leave my sister and go to Spain to join his Spanish Contessa lover who he had recently met.

Marcelle will never forgive me for having been in France twice and not gone to see our poor sister Salomèe. I was ill. I could have gone if I could have taken her home with me, but life is not like that. My mother's voice? My heart is broken a little bit more, but there will be another time, I hope, I wish. I will return.

I have a photograph of Salomèe taken in 1965 by Harry Youlden. One night he came to the Balzac and told my husband Georges that he was a photographer. Georges asked Harry to show him his work and out of the millions of people in Paris, one photograph was that of my sister Salomèe on one of her rare out-ings, looking so sad. Another photo, just as coincidental, was of Hermia Boyd's sister Clytie in London, who we knew well. Deep in my heart I keep imagining my sister Salomèe has died and my sister Marcelle keeps her silence to punish me. Sometimes I paint a little skeleton in my work. Is it a sign? Just *memento mori* probably.

I am sitting in Cicciolina in St Kilda; two gentlemen share their wine with me. I tell them I am working but it doesn't look like it. They are sitting at the table near me and are happily talking. I can't make out what their work is. They talk about various people's characters, two words jump to my ears: 'management' and 'communication'. I'll just keep drinking their wine as I write in a little exercise book with my Cartier pen, who I call La Pompadour. Nice and smooth on the paper and not swallowing ink as some do.

It is 1952, I have been to Georges department store in Collins Street. I am in a train from Melbourne to McKinnon, a man is trying to touch my breasts, he is sitting in the seat opposite me. No one else is in the carriage. It is most unpleasant. I am still wearing a little black Parisian suit and it is early afternoon.

Years later, I am at the Melbourne Club and I rinse my eyes in ex-Prime Minister McMahon's eyes. He is a very intelligent man. Then I rinse my eyes in McEwen's, the leader of the Country Party, that same night. He has hard eyes that never leave me but are also very intelligent. At Violet Dulieu's gallery I rinse my eyes in Arthur Caldwell's. Caldwell looks at me and says I am too intelligent. What a funny man, I think. I have rinsed my eyes in many great men's eyes. Gough Whitlam's at breakfast, at Bermagui. A great man, what could I say to catch his attention? Describe the different sounds of planes which came to bomb Paris when I was a child of eleven. The hum of the American planes, the hum of the English planes, the hum of German planes. Each had a different sound. Mr Whitlam was most intrigued that I recognised the different sounds and their origins. Then I said the word 'Bosnia' and received the history of that land from 1453 to the present. It was wonderful as I happened to have just read *Le Siège la prise et le sac de Constantinople par les Turcs en 1453*, by Gustave Schlumberger. I do read strange books on history.

A great encounter: Neilma Gantner buys my first artwork in 1954 and John Reed is so pleased. Neilma is related to Sunday Reed. My eyes fall into my first lover Allan Wynn's eyes at a party – in his house. The 'click' between eyes is very rare, it is an affinity, usually with a member of the opposite sex. Later, D.L. touches my nipples ever so softly as we play 'Rock Around The Clock' right through the night at 9 Collins Street. We are sitting on my legendary mattresses on the floor, which we used instead of chairs. The art critic Alan McCulloch enters the studio the morning after and I am still in my pyjamas, standing on three mattresses piled on top of one another. Alan McCulloch does not blink an eye. He has come to look at the works on the walls and it is 9 Collins after all – and the first time for him to come to the studio to look at an exhibition of paintings.

Sweeney Reed insists right through an evening at Tolarno that I come and join his table and meet the art critic G.R. Lansell. They had all been at Les Kossatz' exhibition opening at Sweeney's gallery. Exhilaration in the air. John Sinclair talks to me right through the night at the Rudducks' party in St Kilda Road. Georges Mora's voice asking, 'Who wants to play ping-pong?' Martin Sharp, who is kind to my son Philippe in London in 1967. Andrew Sibley, who later worked on *Tympanum* with me, looking delicious. Maurice Chevalier so sweet, telling me I am a good person and that is why he comes to the Balzac almost every day. There would have been no studio at 9 Collins Street if I had not met Molly Douglas on the plane from New York, if she had not been a friend of Colin Wainwright, who found the studio for me.

The actor Melvyn Douglas enjoys the Mora family and friends and the Mirka Café and keeps all his weekends for us. We hear about Hollywood. There were parties at Heide for the very few. Marcel Marceau came to Heide, to the delight of John and Sunday.

Those great art collectors Marc and Eva Besen's last great bouquet of flowers, sent to my husband Georges as he lies dying. He asks, 'Who sent the flowers?' I say, 'Marc and Eva Besen,' and he repeats, very slowly, 'Marc and Eva.' His brain, invaded by cancer, tries desperately to take this in. I am holding his thin arm, two days before his death in the hospice. I am crying. I tell Georges that I am crying and he smiles and later falls asleep. As I watch his bag of urine hanging at the side of his bed, some urine enters the bag and Georges smiles in his sleep – still close to death the *fascinum* has a little pleasure urinating, just like little babies smile in their prams in the sun, asleep, no nappies and wee-wee comes out, causing pleasure.

I just ordered a calvados and shouted two to the charming men who shared their wine with me. Fair is fair in good drinking. The calvados is an apple brandy made in Basse-Normandie. The two gentlemen had never tasted it before. I've changed to my Flaubert pen but the ink has gone. Now I write with my drawing pen. It is the 1998 Writers Festival in Melbourne, and tomorrow I shall go and mingle with all the people at the Malthouse.

People I have talked to and never seen again, but they write to you. All the people who sent me flowers when I was fighting cancer at the Royal Women's Hospital. So many flowers which talk to you through vibrant colours. I did get well, thanks to everybody. People I love – people who make you tremble with fear because you know what a war can do to their persona and turn them into murderers. Am I a murderer too? Yes, I say – I discovered it holding my first child so lovingly and thinking if a person came to take my child, I would have to kill that person. A terrible horror floating about my bed in a lovely 16th arrondissement birth clinic in Paris, 1949. I am twenty-one and the war has ended and Paris is torn apart politically.

The two men sitting next to my table have left; we have exchanged first names and they will buy my memoirs, so they say. Enmeshed in writing, I am walking in quicksand.

In the meantime, my paints are waiting for me and it is time to tackle a new canvas.

I miss Michael Dransfield, the poet. Geoffrey Dutton had sent him to me three years before Michael's death in 1973. Melbourne was then the only place where heroin addicts could get methadone, and only one doctor would care. Michael had already published three books. He carried his father's letters to him in his shirt pocket, on his chest. He was a magic man struggling with death. It was a great honour to be able to give him a home for a while and a taste of peace and art. Once, when I took him yet again to Spencer Street Station, as he climbed into the train I almost went away with him. It was 1972. Imagine being in a train with a poet, going away nowhere, never to return. But I didn't, as I recognised insanity visiting me. It was touch and go and gone. I returned home with a ticket Michael gave me, he knew I loved tickets from train journeys to nowhere.

After Michael died, Mrs Elspeth Dransfield, Michael's mother, came to see me. With her manner and presence, it could have been the mother of Flaubert talking to me intently and listening to me. When I was a little girl, I had a recurring dream after having been to Versailles, aged eight or nine. *La galerie des glaces* had a big impact on me. The dream was right up in the sky, a grand salon like the Versailles *galerie des glaces*, and I was shaking hands of great men and great women: Gustave Flaubert, Napoléon, Victor Hugo, Marie Curie, the Empress Joséphine, and Leonardo's Mona Lisa who I loved. A long row of famous beings and I never forgot the dream.

Meeting the parents of my daughter-in-law, Lucy, was a great event. Entering with your genes into a great family. By now, my six grand-children have Scottish, Irish, English, Australian and American ancestors and I am very pleased.

I am wearing high heels. I am at the Tolarno Gallery; Jimmy Stewart has just come and he is very tall, but so nice and his voice runs all over me. Pierre Cardin has come to look at my work. It's

1967 and he's on his way to Japan. Eyes, more eyes, printing themselves in my brain. No wonder I catch them in my paintings and they remain familiar. Women's eyes are more elusive and harder to catch but you can, and my eyes become more elusive when painted. They give life, as my little mother said.

In 1979 I had not seen my poor mother for twenty-nine years. We wrote to each other almost every week, sometimes more. As I would pass a post office, I would go in and write and post the letter at once. Then, in 1979, a letter came from my sister Marcelle saying that Mother was to be operated on and could die. I had fourteen hours to get to my mother before the operation. I arrived the night before with the help of my husband Georges, who bought air tickets and renewed my passport. My mother always said that I would come to see her when it snowed in the fall (it never does in Connecticut).

The day I arrived, my mother was looking through the window of her hospital room. She looked so small and it was snowing! It hadn't snowed in the fall for fifty-two years – Mother was right again. Next morning, my mother was operated on, for cancer above her coccyx.

I stayed until she came back to her little house, where I remained a little longer. I was regressing terribly, hearing my mother in pain and remembering, as a child, the same sounds she made to express her pain then. What caused that pain? I wondered. My sister Marcelle forbade everyone to say the word 'cancer'. But my mother knew she had cancer. Seeing me naked and looking at my tummy, she started to scream, saying, 'Mirka has the same thing as me.' How could she know then? Fifteen years later I did get cancer, in my womb.

I had to return to Melbourne and didn't know when would be the best time to leave my mother. Would the afternoon be good? No. Would the morning? Would the evening? I could not decide. Finally, I thought I would leave at 4am when it was still night and the sky was full of stars.

Mother always had the light turned on, day and night. As I left for the airport by car, I could see the light in my mother's bedroom window staring at me, like one of the stars in the dark sky above my mother's house.

My mother died six months later from a heart attack, after taking a frozen chicken out of the fridge and holding it tightly against her chest. She had been playing cards with her two nieces Dina and Eveline. She loved chickens, ducks and geese. She hated lobsters, and once in hospital saw them crawling on her wall after taking some tough medicine.

Her second husband was a farmer who had thousands of chickens and ducks and geese and he died of old age. Her third marriage was to a man who read prayers very well in the synagogue. He had suffered as he had previously married a woman who was really a man, and when this person died his sister-in-law took his house and he was left homeless on the street. Mother, being in her own way a very religious person, married him to please God. It was to be a very happy marriage until Mother decided to go and play bingo too often, and her husband became jealous and died pitifully.

Each time Mother remarried, she would write to me, 'Please don't tell Daddy I am getting married again.' During her days in hospital my mother said to me, 'I have done everything wrong. I should have gone to university.'

'Well, Maman,' I said, 'I was born.'

She smiled. She was eighty-two years old and she had survived Hell.

My sister Marcelle was very possessive of her mother, and her two sons, Craig and Marc, loved their grandma. It made me a little jealous as I watched them around my mother so lovingly, so attached. By now I was a stranger, visiting, so disconnected, and had to be brave to resume my own life in Melbourne, my beloved city – my work, my family and a man I loved, a land I could not give up, and irreplaceable friends.

It is 1st September 1998. The first day of spring. Here I am in the tradition of many writers, sitting yet again in a café (this time at Becco), with a Campari and a coffee, ready to organise my next pêle-mêle: my dolls, my teddy bears, my prams, my painting boxes – wood and metal – and my 1928 Windsor & Newton book.

Bears – Paris, 1936. I am holding my teddy bear, which has a doll's head and a furry body and ears like that of a bear. My mother seems to buy too many wafers, I think in my little child's head. My two little sisters are in a big black pram; sometimes Mother puts me in the pram as well and I am ecstatic with pleasure as it feels so good inside. It is dark and cosy in the pram and three little children fit in easily. The smell of the wafers, so sweet and chocolate-scented, mixes nicely with the baby smell that still lingers in the pram.

Bears have to have an expression on their face that I can't resist in order for me to buy them. A message from the unknown maker goes straight to my heart and imagination. The Australian teddies of the thirties are very expressive. I am trying to remember the French ones of that time but because of my doll-teddy my memory is locked, I can't remember French teddies. There are a lot of books on teddy bears now, as people collect them, and I keep looking at the thirties French teddies in these books, but no recollections of any of my own so far.

I sleep in winter with a big French teddy, like the one Shirley Temple had. I bought mine at Georges of Collins Street, and I would have seen it as a child in the famous photo of Shirley Temple and the white bear who is the same as mine, and so big it has annihilated all the smaller ones in my memory. I was an avid film-goer as a child and saw all the Shirley Temple films. There was no school on Thursday afternoons or Saturday afternoons in Paris so Mother put us in the cinema twice a week. The stills outside the cinema would fascinate me, all black and white. I would look at these until Mother came to collect us after the films had ended. I saw all the Buster Keaton, Laurel and Hardy, Charlie Chaplin, and Three Stooges films, and one about the First World War which I have never forgotten. There were soldiers dying in the mud and bad water from a fountain which they were not supposed to drink, but they did and died in a little French village in the film.

The Steiff teddy bears are rare but sometimes reproductions are made of famous ones, like Teddy Rose, made in 1925. This could be bought in Melbourne in the mid-nineties and was quite expensive. I gave Teddy Rose to my granddaughter Lily, with a book in which Teddy Rose is featured. I gave my other granddaughter, Madeleine, a brown and white teddy. I miss him.

Real prams and dolls' prams still send me into rapture. The act of putting dolls in a pram, back on my bed and back into the pram – I can spend literally hours that way recollecting my children and being a mother and a granny. My pleasure never ends and I am puzzled by my behaviour, but I call it working. Working at recapturing past moments printed in my brain and perhaps in other parts of my body, triggered by pleasure in the nervous system's memory.

Many doll collectors acquire prams of all sizes. Once I was bidding for a pram similar to one in a photograph I was given by an elderly lady from whom I had bought a doll. Could it be the same pram? The photo is dated 1910. At that auction I also bid for a doll's dresser against a man and I felt awful when he desisted bidding. I don't know how to bid quietly, I jump out of my seat with both arms in the air, one holding my number on a card so everyone can see me, especially the auctioneer. I can't keep a poker face. That's not exactly the way to behave at an auction. I like to get what I want and usually I need it for my work, which depends upon recollecting — retrieving memories, endlessly, anytime, anywhere, relentlessly.

Painting boxes also drive me crazy. I have wooden ones, black metal ones; the most recent I've bought are Windsor & Newton, and Lefranc. I have some Rembrandt boxes which I use for oil pastels and watercolours. It feels good to have your materials in order. I have a rare book that a charming man gave me. He was an antique dealer many years ago. The book is a 1928 catalogue of all Windsor & Newton's boxes and materials, all I love and desire, all the way from Rathbone Place, London, to Melbourne and my studio.

As a child in the country, I loved watching cows chewing green grass and couldn't understand why the milk was white instead of green. I also loved their long eyelashes and their tails moving all the time, chasing flies. On holidays, Paulette would take me to a little farm to see the cows being milked and I would drink a bowl of warm milk just out of the cow and taken from the bucket. The bulls were elegant and scary, especially if you were wearing something red.

It is 1959 – I am holding my baby Tiriel in my arms. William walks beside me in John and Sunday Reed's fields when their young bull rushes towards me. I am petrified but William chases the bull away with a stick and I am amazed at the courage of William, just six years old. The bull turns around and goes away.

Paris. *Les petits lits blancs*, I am in one of them, my mother and Paulette are standing at the end of the bed, looking at me. My bed sheets are covered with blood, I have just had my tonsils out and am five or six years old. I am standing on the end of the hospital bed. Mother has come to take me home, she dresses me in new clothes. My head is shaven, no hair under my little hat. A sailor's hat with a red pompom.

In 1955, another party at 9 Collins Street. The historian Louis Green comes with a punnet of strawberries, the first I have seen in Melbourne. We are standing on the stairs of the little room at the end of the studio leading to the kitchen and shower room; people are arriving endlessly. It is extraordinary how you can freeze a moment in time for it to stay in your head forever – was it the red of the strawberries or the handsome man, his story or his quality? Probably all of it. Also the perpetual movement of people coming into the studio, upping the tempo.

Sam Angelico just passed by Becco and came in to say hello. His eyes are shiny and he knows all the secrets of Houdini. I met Sam Angelico first at Cliff Pugh's place for my surprise sixtieth party.

Sam was the magician. Hat and doves. Poor Cliff wanted to celebrate my sixty-fifth and seventieth but passed away at sixty-five, but
not before having stolen a kiss on my lips at a Moët et Chandon
opening. A man is a man. He thought he knew where the G-spot
was, but he didn't know.

The novelist Sally Morrison and I, at a dinner in a very nice
restaurant, got a lecture on the G-spot by Cliff, and a very nice
conversation it was. The three of us did drawings as a kind of
bravura. I found out where the G-spot is in an article, 'The Truth
About Women', by Susan Williamson and Rachel Novak in *New
Scientist*, 1st August 1998. I also listened to *The Science Show* on
Radio National, to Doctor Helene O'Connell, a urologist at the
Royal Melbourne Hospital, who inspired the article and told all and
sundry where the G-spot is. The surgeon had a lovely shy, joyous
voice, also telling us about the clitoris being larger than we have
been told to believe. I am still smiling. There is a new book about
the clitoris by Federico Andahazi, called *The Anatomist*.

I think I met Sam Angelico much earlier at Geelong Grammar
School with Barry Kosky, who had his students in rapture, all listening to him talking about Shakespeare *en plein air*. Three poor
artists earning a crust before great times ahead.

At 9 Collins Street a little river ran under the shower room and at
night many slugs would come awalking. Often, half asleep, I
would tread on a slug. One night when I came down, I turned on
the light to look at the floor and saw a big mother slug with five
little babies sliding behind their mother's silver path. A lovely
sight. The wonders of nature. I decided to keep the slugs' domain
and was more careful about where I put my naked feet, always

switching the light on. The slugs told me that water was still under the studio.

The light in the lane used to shine in the studio on all the light parts of my large charcoal drawings that I was doing at the time, between 1959 and 1963. My baby Tiriel was in his cot downstairs so that he wouldn't wake the other two children sleeping upstairs. Many a time, as daylight came, I would be feeding my baby and observing the big charcoal drawings, eight by twelve feet. I worked on these panels again many years later.

Wherever I go now, everyone asks me about the book and gives me advice. Most men say, 'You have to tell all, the smells, the blood, the unbearable.' Women look at me not too sure if I will betray womanhood or not. Some writers ask how I am going, other writers keep a distance from me. Actors are kind, like Tracy Harvey who always stops me and talks to me from her emerald-green bike. But she is a comic, so when she looks straight at me I feel like a little plant that bends but does not break, like in the tales of La Fontaine: the little weed bending by the wind. When comics are serious that's when you have to beware, they could squash you like a moth. I was interviewed once by a New Zealand personality renown for her talent as a comic. The more serious she was, the more I tried to be funny, and the more funny she was, the funnier my seriousness sounded. I have never been able to be serious again in an interview; it sounds funny peculiar. When I was interviewed in French for *Paris Match* in 1997, my French seriousness was even more funny than me trying to be serious in English. Maybe I should speak Latin and roar with laughter. The mind always tricks you and has a great sense of humour when you plot to outdo it.

By now, I have torn away many pages written in earnest but which reread sound totally idiotic. *Vanitas vanitum*. People who are not writing and who do not read but know I am writing look at me with wonder, and those who collect books have already asked me to autograph a copy of mine. They are the true collectors of beautifully made books: *caprices d'érudit*.

I suddenly remember des Esseintes, the hero of Joris-Karl Huysman's *Against Nature*. Looking at his books in a passionate way.

I am having a chowder at David Jones. Last time I came to have a chowder, Quenton Madden was there, alone. I remember first meeting her at a kind of ball, she wore a red dress and was just back from a safari. I was keeping company to John Reed who didn't dance. I was very worried about the safari at the time, and though it was at least thirty years ago, Quenton remembered my reaction to her going on a safari in Africa and assured me she didn't kill any animals. Then or now. She was and still is a stylish woman, very beautiful and poised. *Elle a quelque chose*, as we say in French about an interesting person. She commissioned me to complete a work that she hung above her bed – a butterfly. She had fabulous big diaries of her nineteenth-century ancestors going to buy horses. Their quality and price. I was most impressed as I like early Melbourne history of any aspect. Those diaries, being so reminiscent of the nineteenth century, make me think of the illustrations in *The Dictionary of Australian Artists: Painters, Sketchers, Photographers and Engravers to 1870*, edited by Joan Kerr.

Later, I met Quenton again at my son William's wedding to Lucy and found out that it was Quenton who had introduced

Lucy's mother Cassie to Michael Osborne, her future husband, thereby giving me two grandchildren. How mysterious encounters can be with their consequences, like a whirlwind. Years ago, friends and cousins joined up to buy a painted doll I had made for a birthday girl who came to Rankins Lane, where I lived, to collect her doll. That young girl was Lucy Osborne. I can still see her floating through my studio. Little did I know that this beautiful girl would become my daughter-in-law.

Peter Beilby, a friend of William's, married Lucy's cousin Melly. In 1987 Charles Blackman had a show in Sydney and William, who was staying with Melly, asked Lucy if she would like to go to the opening. She did. Three days later, Lucy arrived in Melbourne with a little suitcase full of toys and moved in with William in his new gallery at Windsor Place in the city.

How our parents move and we are born. More stories in LA. More stories in Lisbon. More stories in Paris. More stories in Melbourne. More stories in New York. Well, it's time to buy more ink to feed my five pens and sneak into my house two new canvases who will wait and soothe me as I write a little more, a little longer, gnawing away at my brain.

Photographs are appearing and this is devastating me. Photographs are so poignant and sound louder than screams in your mind. I remember reading Roland Barthes' *La Chambre claire: Note sur la photographie*. My son William bought the book in Paris for me in May 1980. My son Philippe had given me the large Eugène Atget book, *Paris*. I am hypnotised by photographs. I hear them breathing, I hear the camera, I see the moment *figé* forever, the streets of Paris pierce my heart. The soul of the photographed person lasts forever; the young never age, and the old smile forever or stare painfully forever. The photographer as a *maître de cérémonie*.

I only know my maternal grandparents, Myer and Mirka Gelbein, through a photograph I adore, taken in 1920. I saw a photograph, as a child, of my twelve aunts, each more beautiful than the next – my father's elder sisters. They all wore peaked caps and long trousers. In 1938 I saw a photograph of my paternal grandmother, also old-looking like my maternal grandmother, even though they were only forty-two and forty-three years old. Once, in Melbourne, a man rang us to say that his parents had been to the wedding of Georges Mora's parents and he had old photos. He gave us the pictures and we lost track of him. He was a bureaucrat. He was also a bridge player and had read the obituary of Georges' mother, who was a bridge player in Portugal and later in New York. The obituary said that Georges' mother had a son who lived with his family at 9 Collins Street in Melbourne, a very famous street. A beautiful story.

And now, in 1998, my dearest friend Geoffrey Dutton has died and I am so sad. But poets and writers never really die, their voices trot along our path to give us courage to treasure our life, again, for a little while. I read Geoffrey's work to soothe my grief, his poems, his autobiography, his letters. I read *Old Melbourne Memories*, written in 1884 by Rolf Boldrewood, also to soothe my grief. I read Simone de Beauvoir's *Beloved Chicago Man* to soothe my grief and remember Paris of 1947. I go from one book to another and think how precious our poets and writers are. I think, as I always have, I find peace in a book. Simone de Beauvoir's English also soothes me as her *tournures de phrases* are not unlike mine, thinking in French and writing in English, so that my prose is somehow demanding.

Today, 25th September 1998, James Smeaton has a show at William
Mora Galleries. Last time, James and I shared a show in Sydney at
Mary Place Gallery. My son William had hired the space for us.
James came to my hotel before the show, he could see a little breakdown eating me up, normal for me before a show. He is a true artist
and probably rescued me from my torments by talking to me so
gently and knowingly. I had not shown in Sydney for thirty years and
it was a total sell-out, a great success. I had been honoured with great
interviews in the newspapers and on radio. James's work is about life
and death on an equal footing and his colours are speaking to my
soul, they are like Giotto's angels. If they would only appear.

An extract from a diary begun in 1994:

> *Boulevard de Charonne, 1936. Premier étage, une chambre et
> cuisine et alcôve au-dessus d'un bal-musette.* Father is ironing
> coats my mother has sewn together. My Aunt Mimi also helps.
> I pull out the tacking in white threads. Across the courtyard a
> woman lives with a little boy, Serge, who is my age. On the
> same floor a little child cries in his cot and the room smells of
> urine when the door is left open onto the landing. My sisters
> and I go to the toilet outside on the landing and look at each
> other, the parts where we wee, then go home again. A little
> ritual for a few days. Father has come one day and it is so nice
> and quiet. He has promised Mother to be good. Mother has a
> new bed and mattress.
>
> One day, Father brings live eels for dinner in a brown
> paper bag. Father drops the bag and all the eels go under the
> beds and table. Father and Mother have to crawl to get the eels

back and there is much merriment from the children. Marcelle is showing the new mattress to my father. Marcelle walks at night in her sleep and Mother caught her the other night on the window sill about to fly out, all over Paris. At night I sleep in a makeshift bed in the kitchen. I hear Mother say, 'Not yet, the children are not asleep.' So I listen and my parents make strange noises, the bed creaks.

Downstairs the *bal-musette bat son plein*. My father is really good and not bad-tempered. I have to go and buy the newspapers every day, every two hours. Father is reading and showing me the long speeches of Hitler. A bad man. In the paper *Paris Soir* war is in the air and yet it is springtime; the little *communiantes* outside in the street are like white butterflies. I have to put the bread outside as it is *Pesser* and it is *Matzos* time.

I have a good report from school and come first every month. Mother and her sister talk about me. I have a girlfriend at school called Nadine who is related to a famous actress, Alida Valli. My sister Salomèe is at La Rochelle in a sanatorium. Madame Brainne and her daughter Micheline have arrived, they told my father where to find us, they are the friends of Mother and Father since always. Mother has left several times with her three little girls, it is another try again. Next time it will be 1950 when Mother goes for good to America and divorces my dad.

Early memories are of 214 rue de Crimée when I am four or five years old and Paulette lives across the road and I wave at her, she waves back. One day, I am in the street somehow, she kneels in front of me and gives me a Rocher chocolate, which is delicious. Mother watches. Thus starts a great love, she is twenty-five years old and a journalist. She loves a man who is married, she smokes English cigarettes – Players – and blows lovely rings of smoke for me. Together, they sing opera duets to me when I am at Paulette's place on the weekend. It is another Easter and Roger, Paulette's lover, brings me a large chocolate chicken with lots of little eggs full of liqueur which fill the chicken's tummy. Every Saturday afternoon, Paulette sleeps in her bed while the radio plays classical music. I play quietly on the carpet with silver coins. Sometimes, I look through the windows and see rooms with people partying on different floors. Every Sunday in good weather we go to Garches to do *culture physique*. Henri is the teacher. He gives me red cherries sometimes. Paulette is to marry him later, after asking me who she should marry. I told her Henri, knowing that she could not get Roger. A child is cunning sometimes.

I have started this diary on Easter Monday 1994, after seeing the film about Ingmar Bergman's parents. It was so evocative and interesting to imagine your parents before you were born and when you were a little child. But parents remain a mystery.

On 13th October 1998 the Lord Mayor and councillors of the City of Melbourne award the title of Honoured Artist to Mirka Madeleine Mora 'in recognition of lifelong achievement in the arts which has made an outstanding contribution to the life of this city'. (Lord Mayor Ivan Deveson AO.) This is a great honour and I must be over seventy, thinking yet I have another full life waiting for me – I dream. But mortality is there and to face it bravely one must cherish every minute of life and people, and continue to paint and study and be bewitched by this unfathomable universe we live in. Charles Tingwell, the actor, and Albert Tucker, the painter, are the two other artists honoured.

After a week of being disconnected and very moved, I am back to my own self and very honoured and moved always.

My cat Pompom and I are in an *Age* interview on 21st October 1998, about my house. A young writer, Hugh Martin, conducted the interview without blinking an eye, and a young photographer, Penny Stephens, got Pompom at his best behaviour, offering himself. A good trooper. An interview is a performance and I do love it and am honoured every time. Usually I am slightly outrageous and, as I have been told, make good copy.

As I lift my eyes to look at my cart, which is covered with books by now, I see a book I could not find this morning. It is *Magical Nights at the Theatre* by Charles Waller, 1854–1948, who performed in Melbourne. In it is one of my favourite pictures, Houdini jumping off Queen's Bridge into the Yarra River, Melbourne, 17th February 1910. It was at lunch hour and twenty thousand people watched. There is also, on the opposite page, an aeroplane flight description. 'Houdini in the air sustained flight at Digger's Rest. Report of first sustained aeroplane flight made in Australia, 18th March 1910.'

This autobiography is like a neverending story. I feel like Scheherazade *dans les mille et une nuits* trying to save my life. The trouble is I can't remember how Scheherazade ends. As I walked towards the sea three days ago, 28th October 1998, I noticed the face at the entrance to Luna Park had been unrobed and the moon-man face of 1912 had appeared. For the last three days I have gone to photograph the face from all angles. The eyes are painted in a primitive way, shaky lines around the irises: it is two years before the Great War, they are sad. The face is many layers of papier mâché over wire. The eyebrows are plaster and I am berserk about it. The painting effect of old frescoes – the Renaissance ones – disintegrating.

Inside Luna Park the merry-go-round is also dismantled and it is summertime. I am in disarray. As I watch the passers-by looking at the moon man it is the children who react passionately, proud to differentiate the old face from the new one gone. Some people take photographs of people under the moon face. I have many photographs now of the moon man. When I look at the whites of his eyes, they look concave; when I turn the picture upside down, the whites look convex. It is all very uncanny. Our eyes amuse themselves at our expense as we grow older and are on the alert, vigilant. But we must die and leave lots of messages. Good clues for hopefully the happiness of a good world on the little earth, like an epithalamium.

In Saint-Quay-Portrieux Georges and I played our game of ping-pong outside in the sun. I watched Georges being very agile and with all sorts of fun expressions. Very jolly and happy and sunburnt. At a certain time he was too hot and took his jumper off and put it on the chair quickly so as to resume our game, but I stopped to go to the chair to fold the jumper nicely and then back to the ping-pong game for a little while. Folding the jumper was my way of seducing Georges, but once we were married I never folded his clothes.

In Paris, 1947–48: crossing a street and the great theatre man Charles Dullin crossing the street towards me. One evening, as Georges and I take a stroll, we stop at a merry-go-round and there is Jean-Paul Sartre watching also the same merry-go-round. And a little child. Coming out of 51 rue Eugène Carrière an open car passes rapidly; in it is a young Jean Marais with a big Alsatian dog. Jean Marais at the wheel, his blond hair flowing in the wind. He was the great love of Jean Cocteau. Having lunch at the Grand

Véfour: the waiter is bringing a little stool for my feet as I am with child. We eat the finest *haricots verts*, who melt in your mouth. Recently, Philippe Mouchel of Langton's had succeeded in having some grown and given me one to taste. It was delicious. At the restaurant in rue Caulaincourt where we have a *fontainebleau* for a sweet, the waiter comes with a large glass jar with *crème Chantilly* and one with the light *fromage blanc*, to mix together.

On my wedding night we go to dinner, quite late, at Chez Madame Arthur in rue Lepic. All the men wear lipstick. We buy in a shop fresh *moules*, mussels, by the litre. We love the orange mushrooms, the *chanterelles brunes*, the *cèpes de Bordeaux*, we take them home and cook them *à la minute, au beurre*, with garlic and parsley. The mussels in white wine, parsley, onions, pepper, fresh cream, all *à la minute*: always in a hurry, we have to go dancing or hear Juliette Gréco, Edith Piaf. Theatres, ballets, concerts and films, and Georges disappears again to work and I worship his photograph near my bed. I paint small pictures. There is a very nice old man who looks at me with piercing eyes when I go to his shop to buy paints, brushes and heavenly little canvases with copper nails to pin the canvas on the wood. He knows many things that I don't. His way of smiling tells me that.

We go to the very famous Swimming Pool Lepecq. By then, we have a little boy, Philippe. Once, Georges jumps into the swimming pool and knocks a man on his head. *C'est Jean-Louis*. The man is an old friend of Georges from his days in the Foreign Legion. He has a wife, Marie-Jeanne, who is a mannequin at Paquin. We renew a great friendship and play every week canasta, all night in each other's homes, in turn. We always take our baby. The lamplights in the street fascinate my little baby, who opens his eyes wide in the night, safe in his pram.

In the daytime, after the birth of Philippe, when the *femme de ménage* we share with Marie-Jeanne and her husband comes, I go often to watch seahorses swimming in a shop on the Champs Elysées. The *femme de ménage* tells me the goings on in Marie-Jeanne's marriage when she goes away to Lyon, where her parents have a famous restaurant and Jean-Louis is bringing bouquets of flowers. 'Now, who are the bouquets for?' the *femme de ménage* says. Suite medleys.

Time goes very fast in Paris. We read Kafka's diary; Georges always buys the books just printed. We can't pass a library without capturing the latest books. *L'Etranger* by Camus, *La Peste*, *La Chute*, *Noces*, *Le Mythe de Sisyphe*. *The Flies* and *No Exit* by Sartre. Charles Morgan, Julien Green. *Le Deuxième Sexe* by Simone de Beauvoir. Koestler, Gide, so many books to read. Films to see: *Le Diable au corps*, starring Micheline Presle and Gérard Philippe, directed by Autant-Lara. Violette Leduc's *l'Affamée* is another book to read. In Paris, as in every city, one reads the newspapers daily. In Parisian papers, articles often are written by great writers and we become very engaged reading it all. Coming out of the war, I am very puzzled that so many issues are still argued – surely it is bad to be a fascist?

The French communist party is confusing. De Gaulle is very confusing. I always want to be on the side of the people in the street. Reading *Le Sang des autres – The Blood of Others* – by de Beauvoir. *Les Jeux sont faits*. The chips are down. I still have all these old books! All paperbacks. *L'Eté*, by Camus, I bought in Melbourne in 1954, a book written in 1939. I wanted it in Paris in 1948. Had to wait. I am rereading it in 1999. It is amazing the memory of books one has and slowly loses, but the memory of a writer, its soul, one never loses and it is a good, invisible companion following you through life. Albert Camus is one of those writers glued to my soul.

When I was young I read passionately *Journal politique*, two volumes by Comte Galeazzo Ciano, *éditeur* Oreste Zeluck. My maiden name is Zelik. How intriguing the names we carry – are they related? I read feverishly *The German Generals Talk*, by B.H. Liddell Hart. *L'univers concentrationnaire de Rousset*. My reading has always been in all directions but somehow I have some treasures I find instinctively and which are always useful for my growth as a painter and human being.

It is Melbourne, 18th December 1998. I shall reread Camus' *L'Eté* for a while and leave my writing, it is 12.20pm. A few hours of reading will make me hungry and force me to eat something. So I go to Oran with Camus. *Ville somnambule et frénétique*: Camus described Oran in 1939 as a lover describes his mistress.

Back on the page at 5pm and I am crying with emotion as I realise how much work I still have to do to capture the book. Christmas wishes from my publisher makes the book real. I usually try to escape reality but this time I am *coincée*, cornered; *le minotaure* smiles at me. All I can hope is for another tomorrow to write a little more and enrich the text I have grabbed this year, day after day from October 1997 to October 1998. Then I lose the spell of the discipline and decide to read more to go back into writing, thinking, Reading is to my brain what swimming is to an athlete swimmer. Although I am ecstatic when I write, I do find any excuse to push away the moment of going back to my desk. My brain is like a cat in a garden full of butterflies and grasshoppers and crickets.

The sun has set and I am in Saint-Paul-de-Vence in 1992, where I'm
conducting a workshop. My student and friend Joy is with me sitting
at a table in a perfect restaurant, where everything is perfect: the tables,
the chairs, the waiter, the light. Somehow all the other students are
behind a big wall dining somewhere else. The restaurant is on top of
the hill, the landscape is ready to go to sleep, all is quiet and I cannot
capture the moment, it is too beautiful. *Il faut donc me résigner et vivre
ce moment sans mots*. The restaurant is called La Couleur Pourpre.

I think the name Mirka might come from the word *mercado*,
meaning in Spain and Spanish countries a market, a marketplace; a
painter is a kind of marketplace. Words are tools to catch my brain
where recently the minotaur has come to take me on a merry dance.
King Minos was married to Pasiphaë who gave birth to the minotaur, half man and half bull. Pasiphaë had fallen in love with a bull.
I know a good story about Pasiphaë.

Paris, 1936: wondering for days in front of the pipe of our stove
how Father Christmas could fit into the pipe. It was an incredible
miracle if it was true. I was extremely puzzled and kept thinking
about it, not sharing my puzzlement for many days, with anyone.

I shut all the lights and with a torch near my face looked into the
mirror. There was a Rembrandt, a Caravaggio, a Giorgione. The
shadows smoothed the outlines of my face and I was ecstatic. It is
real art: the soul shines in the dark.

If I am upset, very deeply, the nervous system in my feet
attacks my walking and stops it. If I sort out the problem the pain
goes and I can resume my walking. All pains gone.

The women who love my sons always suffer. Every woman
who has sons could say the same.

I found my copy of George Sand's autobiography. In the photo album are Flaubert and Louis Blanc, whose brother Charles wrote *Grammaire des arts du dessin*. Louis Blanc was the politician who was also close to George Sand for a while. George Sand in *Histoire de ma vie* does not speak about the *tourment de coeur*. She writes, *'l'amitié a sa pudeur comme l'amour a la sienne'*.

Trying to sit on my mother's knees but I have grown too much and it feels uncomfortable. I am sad. The room is full of friends I alone have noticed. I am like a little bird who has fallen out of its nest. I am only twelve and it is summer in Paris.

Number 9 Collins Street's fireplace, the little summer *grillon* – cricket – who spent all the winter there and no one was allowed to chase him away. His song was so feeble in winter but comforting. Each winter a little *grillon* took his lodging with us and sang.

Watching in January 1999 Jonas Bjorkmann and Thomas Muster – great beauty and fierceness in the racket sending the ball. The body and mind at full speed, the crowd silent, full of expectation. Tennis watching helps me to attack my canvas. *Je rugis comme un lion*.

My ears are on the alert, after the injections. The dentist came with his tool to extract my tooth who has split in two. Two centimetres of root detaching itself from the flesh surrounding the bone of the tooth's root. There is an abscess, quite large; as it breaks down, its coolness refreshes, my poor flesh anaesthetised, its liquid like a bird's pee on your neck as it flies over you. Drops of magic as all my body trembles slightly. The blood from my gum is thick like syrupy blackberry juice, a Prussian blue with some alizarin crimson.

Studying the blood makes me forget the animal fear lurking all over my body, still shaking. Watching one's life without participating in it is a bit like being in a theatre and watching a performance. The depth of oneself can only promise bad surprises, and yet if one aimed high one would end a saint or a murderer: nothing in between could attract me, *hélas*, so I remain a watcher of the watcher I am, so it seems. My paintings have more courage than I and deploy the vagaries of my mind, great and small, and give me away every time – no secrets in art, all is *dévoilé*, told, unveiled.

Beware of Pity, a film I saw in the late forties – I also read the novel many times – had an enormous impact on me. It was about unrequited love, written by Stefan Zweig who suicided eventually, with his lover. Unrequited love has always attracted me, as in the end, after much suffering, you remain free to choose another unrequited love or stick to the one you have and study your behaviour and that of your opponent. As you mature, great fun is to be had: in my case, thirty years later I still observe and choose my miseries and pleasures. Such is life; and the paintings remain a mystery, threatening my sanity or saving it at other times. So too with the working of the mind, sometimes treacherous and sometimes elevating – *mais le mystère de l'âme continue*, never to be revealed perhaps? Do I hear a grain of sand telling me a little something? Suddenly I think of Papageno in *The Magic Flute* by Mozart. Sometimes I see Papageno in my painting; Papageno is a bird catcher who pretends he has killed the serpent, but the ladies padlock his lying tongue. I hear bells and the magic flute. Great art is always there to rescue us.

I drink wine with two friends, Donlevy and Phillip. We speak about love and wine and fairness. Donlevy has done a lot to lift St

Kilda as a civilised place, same as my husband Georges and I did with Tolarno in the sixties. Lately I am always older than the beautiful men I love, so I have to dream and drink and talk about our wondrous life instead of . . .

'It seems that Roman people thought that the depiction of the sexual act was the cause of great laughter' – Aristotle, from *Looking at Lovemaking: Constructions of Sexuality in Roman Art, 100BC–AD250*, by John R. Clarke. A beautiful book I am reading.

I am at Donovans on the seaside, the cruel sun is setting on the cruel sea and my cruel stomach is eating a delicious fish who got caught on a line today.

At Metropolis bookshop in Acland Street I meet a live poet, Dorothy Porter. Watching her speaking words, giving birth to her lines yet again, to a story, stories in the form of poems, I wonder how she can resist beautiful prose: a poet must write poems, I think to console myself, poems as a kind of corset to contain crystallised thoughts. What am I saying here – is there anything more poignant than poems? Yes, Nijinski dancing *l'Après-midi d'un faune*, and I could say that Dorothy Porter was almost dancing as she spoke her poems.

Will I or won't I tell the story of Pasiphaë? I think I
have lost my innocence but I usually
regain it.

MY WORK

ne day, Dr Edward de Bono came to my studio and, looking at my dolls, embroideries, charcoals, pen and ink drawings, paintings and pastels, pointed at my dolls and asked me, 'Now, these dolls that you make, are they for your paintings, or are the paintings for the dolls?'

'A perfect question to ask me,' I answered, 'the dolls are for the paintings.'

'This is what I wanted to hear,' said Dr de Bono. Exactly what Maurice Chevalier had replied years before.

My dolls are my drawings in three dimensions; they came about when I started my life alone, in my studio in Wellington Street, St Kilda, 1970. As a rule, I do not paint if I am distressed, I like to have a clear mind. I was extremely distressed, and brave, when I left my family. Because of that distress, I found myself cutting out my drawings, and they looked like the paper dolls I used to play with as a child, particularly the five Dionnes, little quintuplet girls, very famous then, in the thirties.

I also had seen in Max Harris's Mary Martin Bookshop printed dolls on cloth, circa 1910, ready to cut out, sew together, stuff and paint. As I am a compulsive worker and self-taught artist, it was a natural turn of events to cut out my drawings until I clarified my mind, my sorrows, and got myself in hand. It was extremely agreeable to have my drawings transformed into soft sculptures and also to paint them, and hold them in my hands. Of course not every drawing lent itself to a doll. A painting is always a kind of enemy, it gives you a hard time until it exists of its own accord.

As I must have been very lonely, the dolls were a kind of solid dream; I was very enthralled by them. I had two or three exhibitions of these: at Ray Hughes' gallery in Brisbane; at Marianne Baillieu's Realities Gallery in Melbourne; and at Tolarno, River Street, South Yarra in 1983, curated by William and Georges Mora. I could have made a fortune, as people adored them. Alan McCulloch the art critic adored them also, but I thought it was too good a pleasure for one person and decided to do workshops, sharing my knowledge with people, and then slowly go back to my canvases.

The doll workshops were, and are still, extremely popular and a good earner but too great a distraction from my work. My work I call painting. Painting is hard, it leads you to great exaltations and to the deepest despair. *Et pourtant*, there is no other way to exist in my case, and the same applies to many painters. It is very much like searching for the secret of the universe; it does not matter how many theories of colour you know and what you have to say, the road is long to find yet another painting to exalt you again. One progresses very slowly in the handling of paint, which has so many orgasms in reserve.

I am thinking of Michel-Eugène Chevreul's theory of simultaneous contrasts. I am thinking suddenly of John Gage's *Colour and Culture: Practice and Meaning from Antiquity to Abstraction*. I found that book at the Arts Bookshop, where I go secretly as I have an account and big discount at Cosmos, my other bookshop in St Kilda. Sometimes you want a book at once, and I myself don't like to wait for a book as I usually need it for my work. I need books that contain great pieces by art historians in their different fields, their different views on various painters and subjects. Books for me are a kind of departure, an invitation to Cythera. One of my great adventures was to read (and reread and reread) the four volumes of *Studies in Western Art*, which came out of the International Congress on the History of Art.

The story of Erichthonius is intriguing and led me to many drawings and paintings. All the elements of the myth are very enticing to me, very seductive. The story goes like this, more or less: Erichthonius is born with a serpent's tail; he is the son of Gaea the earth goddess, who was impregnated when Hephaestus tried in vain to ravish Athena and his seeds fell on Gaea. The child, guarded by one or two snakes and shaped like a snake, is born from these seeds. In the third volume of *Studies in Western Art*, Wolfgang Stechow has a chapter called 'The Finding of Erichthonius: An Ancient Theme in Baroque Art', in which I saw thirteen renditions by various painters: Rembrandt, Bor, Rubens, an etching by Antonio Tempesta (my favourite), and a few more artists and engravings as well. The child is hidden by Athena in a basket and given to three sisters who are told not to open the basket, but they do and see the wondrous child. Each painter reacted so differently to the child with a serpent's tail. The Rubens sisters caressed the little child, all naked and sensuous. Rembrandt's sisters screamed. My rendition of the story was based on love and wonder and lasciviousness.

Sometimes I think it must be as good to 'read' paintings as to make them. It is uncanny how you encounter a book at the right time and it gives you a great push, a revelation that consolidates your work, your thinking. Sunday Reed gave me *Lettres complètes d'Abélard et d'Héloïse* – her mother's book – *Ouevres poétiques* by Apollinaire, and *The Penguin Book of French Verse*. Charles Blackman gave me the Supervielle book, *Oublieuse mémoire*.

Lovers give you books that you understand later in years, after the affair has ended.

Being self-taught, my reading is very much like a *girouette* and sometimes like a compass. And as I go in all directions, I find my own way to enrich my knowledge of art and the making of it, and, with luck, my thinking. All the same, face to face with a new canvas, it is as if you have never held a brush before, and all the knowledge melts, probably into something marvellous, and you are alone with your work which appears slowly, so slowly, but surely.

Letters and writings from painters are great sources of knowledge and comfort. I think of Matisse on painting, Leonardo da Vinci's notebooks, Van Gogh's letters to his brother Theo, the writings on Poussin, Corot, Vermeer. I could write lists and lists of subjects on painters only, that would cover the earth and the sky.

I also love to spend hours looking at Michael Jaffé's four volumes of *The Devonshire Collection of Italian Drawings*, on the Tuscan and Umbrian schools, Venetian and North Italian schools, Bolognese and Emilian schools, Roman and Neapolitan Schools. By looking at all these works, I discover the different materials used and renew my adoration of drawing, which in turn enriches my paintings.

Many a time I have gone to bed very hungry, but with rare

books as good teachers. Far into the night I read all the mysteries that lines hide, contain or give away. Many clues to the next generations of true artists and connoisseurs of art.

Of course, besides the secret lines there is the sensuality of the shadows and the life of the light, giving volumes to the figures and the *demi-teinte*. I myself love flat figures, but slowly the landscape of this country appears in some of my paintings, as I am a frustrated landscape painter. I would love painting the landscape but that's where my idea of suicide appears. Painting the landscape would shorten my life, take all my soul away to be first a piece of cloth you clean your brushes on; the wind would blow me away in the landscape.

But I am preparing myself to paint a landscape in my very old age and it will be my Australian testament, for I love this country physically; I know how the Aboriginal people read this land and in turn inspire us, who know that we are only passing by with our short life on this earth.

What is intriguing to me about my work is that when I prepare my palette, and I like a very limited amount of colours, I will hear music. High notes for brighter tones or pure colour, and low notes for darker tones or colours – red, brown, black. Got to go back to John Gage's book, especially Chapter 9, 'Colour Under Control: The Reign of Newton'. It describes the palette of great artists, to be read as music in my case, or great novels, *le secret des couleurs*. It is so good to read and see palettes of great masters through the centuries, how colours were thought of, particularly the idea of red, yellow and blue, all explained in the Gage book, along with the origins of the colour circles, which were accidentally devised by physicians when diagnosing disease by uroscopy. But then printers also discovered mixtures of colours by chance.

All the disciplines are a family to produce the making of art. But it is good to have a grandparent's genes who was a painter in any manner in any century. As you can see, talking about my work makes me go round and round, always ending up alone in front of a canvas or a blank page of best paper with best pens and paints. I think when you don't want to be the prisoner of a formula, at each painting you start you have to reinvent the art of painting – it takes more time, and the interest you find in searching gives life to your work. And it shows, for colours are made by our feelings, our optic nerves, our observations of nature that we have to rob, to steal from. Even though nature is offering all her secrets, we still have to decipher it, concoct it as best we can and sometimes reinvent, as her lighting is often treacherous: a sudden violent wind turns all the leaves of the trees from light to dark, and vice versa; the rough sea could blind you with its white foam as it roars.

On very good days, when I am not writing and have no interruptions, I will find myself at my easel not remembering having left my bed. I will work until 3.30pm, stop, have a coffee, a shower, and go out and have lunch, often at Cicciolina in Acland Street. The lunch is really my breakfast, lunch and dinner in one go. Sometimes I love to go to Becco in town, it is close to my son William's gallery. Then I will go back and look at my work, often in total wonder as I know a painting takes in my case many months to achieve. If it is a very good painting, I will hide it so I can look at it for a long time, as I could never afford to buy it – a bit like a dog who hides its bone. Then I have to study my treasured books to find out more about painting. If there is a great show of masters at the National Gallery of Victoria, I will go and lose myself in the rhythm of the brushstrokes and get too excited about the way of the applied colours, go home like a drunken sailor – dangerous.

But it is most important to see good work as I still have to learn so much. In the fifties and sixties, I was surrounded by beautiful painters and their work. I was learning fast, but slow in digesting my learning. John Perceval's flamboyance, Charles Blackman's poetry, Arthur Boyd's naturalness come to mind. Joy Hester's passions, Nolan's magic, Fred Williams crystallising his art. I loved Fred Williams coming to my studio at 9 Collins Street with a little bottle of drawing ink in his pocket and pen and nibs, and drawing my children, my cat Napoléon, and myself brushing my hair. His line was impeccable and I learned about the true art of observing, drawing, seeing and simplicity.

Arthur Boyd was very generous with his paints: he ground them himself and would often bring large tubes to me and to Charles. Once we all got nursery blue and what a blue it was – dreamy. Arthur also sharpened bamboos into fine quills for me to draw with when he noticed my *acharnement* – relentlessness – at drawing. Two other painters I loved watching were John Howley and Don Laycock. I learned about tonal value from them as well as rebellion, colourwise. At John and Sunday Reed's home I would have learned much without knowing as the house was full of paintings and I drank them with my eyes and brain, which of course is good schooling for a self-taught artist, to be surrounded by so many artworks.

Though I love abstract art and get enormous pleasure out of it, I tend to be a maker of images, my eternal images. Eternal because they are so simple – children together, often holding or surrounded by birds or dogs, a sky, a tree, a fence, the faint suggestion of a far-away landscape. Little hills are coming, as I see them at The Four Winds open-air concert every year in Bermagui. I dribble looking at the perfect landscape behind the musicians' stage, and a transparent wall separates them from the little hills and trees and a little lake. The music and landscape is enough gearing for one year or more of paintings. Slowly I will have more courage to go into landscape, even if the price is high for me.

One year, as I was listening to the ensemble Gombert and Fonte play Bach's three motets for double choir, I happened to lift my head and look at the sky, and I realised that I would leave the sky as well as the earth when I die, and I cried miserably. Maybe, when we die, we turn into music if we listen to it carefully when we are alive. I must say the immensity of the sky over Bermagui was so grand that all my emotions got very confused and I was glad for it. It is good to be confused – you can choose your miseries then, and afterwards.

Later, leaving the ensemble, directed by John O'Donnell who had also given us *Venetian Coronation*, it was very hard to bridge my visual scenery of all the doges in their palaces and suddenly go into real life. It was very painful, I was stranded in seventeenth-century Venice.

This reminds me of a book I bought in France in 1992 called *Behind the Image* by Federico Zeri. It is about all the adventures painters and paintings have: how and why they were painted, how some got lost and found again, how painters were inspired or told in ancient times to produce certain subjects and not others. Paintings were sometimes inspired by erudite people, great writers, philosophers, and all the symbols were definitely related to stories or legends and were more familiar then than now to the people. There are beautiful conversations in this magnificent book.

A painting can become a great classical novel, like Brueghel's painting, *La Tentation de Saint Antoine*, which inspired Flaubert to write his novel of the same name. I get great inspiration from Euphrosyne Doxiadis' *The Mysterious Fayum Portraits: Faces from*

Ancient Egypt and I am sure one or more of the portraits could be one of my ancestors. The faces jump out of time and give me endless frissons. I think I hear the sound of their voices, that their eyes see me. The freshness of their rendering is breathtaking. I smell their *chevelures*, feel the hot sun, their exotic perfumes. With all the beautiful works in books and elsewhere, I feed my soul and brain; the mystery of creation remains. I feel very lucky to have been able, all my life, to hang on to my gift of searching and learning about my trade as a painter, even if sometimes I break down the self-control of my dearest friends.

Toys also are a part of my work as they trigger childhood memories that are very embedded in time, and in my mind. All is for my work, to push it further, to think a little better, especially when I have to understand my various behaviours. Toys allow me to make better drawings and paintings, to capture more signs and signals that will precipitate other images.

Recently, I resisted for a month buying a yellow cart one hundred years old, at least. The wheels are big, made of iron. The cart must have been in a shed at a farm, in the bush. A cart does not belong in a house and it was hard for the two men who got it inside for me. I could not understand my fixation for such an odd cart. It is in my writing room and it and I purr together: it has the chapters of my book that I am presently writing, French and English and Latin dictionaries. It has my scrapbook, also the fifth volume of Diderot's *L'Encyclopédie*; a globe of the earth; *Debonair Jack: A Biography of Sir John Longstaff* by Prue Joske; the Jaffé books on the Devonshire collection of drawings; *La Prose française* by Emile Faguet *de l'Académie Francaise*, a large volume but a cuddly shape; a very big box with Faber Castell pastels, *aquarelles*, charcoals, *crayons de couleurs*.

The cart is immensely happy here. Recently, I discovered the reason for my insane obsession with the cart, coming from a little girl Mirka, eight years old. It is Paris, 1936, the big Depression, but we live in a large apartment on the third floor, rue de Crimée. I am alone in the apartment. I look through the window and my heart falls out of me. My father and mother are pulling a little yellow cart, screaming in turn, '*Marchand d'habits – chiffons*,' down the street. My mother would have hated it, my father must have forced her to go with him.

As I write, I am suddenly shaking all over and tears are flowing and I am sobbing. Recollecting myself, I will have to find out why I am trembling and sobbing. I will draw my cart I love so much and maybe an image will tell me more secrets, as I think that often art is also a kind of oracle. *Hélas*, when all is said and done it is still difficult to know how and when a good painting comes. A while ago I heard that pigs have the intelligence of a child of five years old. A lovely painting arrived with a child and an angel holding a pig. I was very pleased with this painting, done recently (got to hide it).

Sometimes at Edelweiss, where I love to have a late lunch, I watch the two handsome owners, Linton and Peter. They are Australians who often choose French-looking *serveuses*, but sometimes a Chinese man works there, and recently a really agile young Aussie man. Faces are as good as landscapes for one's drawing; they are like a theatre play, a bit like in my old restaurants, Balzac, Tolarno and the Mirka Café. I sure have drawn and painted a lot of people, and when I look at my drawings or paintings from the fifties to now, I recognise faces that have passed me by or spoken to me or smiled at me, or faces my eyes rested on. Other times, I think I am painting the same face with its soul, again and again. I keep searching faces printed in my brain a long time ago – was I born with all these? Faces in my genes staring at me. I carry them; faces let me recognise them ever so faintly, like verses you know but have forgotten. As you hear them you have pleasure, something in your memory moves and you recognise the verses. Recently, my friend Carillo recited in French 'The Albatross' by Baudelaire. The verse came towards me, cascading in my brain, saying, Hello! Hello! It was very pleasant and pleasing.

I always thought and still think that words are paintings and drawings in disguise, but is it poetry in disguise or prose in disguise? I am puzzled yet again. Jean François Champollion appears to me with his discovery of the secret of the ancient hieroglyphs of Egypt. I will have to read more as I love both *éperdument*, prose and poetry. Painting appears to me suddenly more magic than ever, as it contains in my humble thinking poetry and prose whose language is universal. Jean Froissart, 1333–1410, enchanted me by his painterly descriptions of his time, of the people, big *batailles*, and daily life. He was a priest who travelled and spent his life writing *des chroniques*. By reading his work one can enter paintings of the time and, if I dare say it, read the palette of the artists in a more intimate way.

It is in moments like this I am very fortunate to be able to look at my large book, *Paintings in the Louvre*, by Lawrence Gowing, and find the school of Paris at Froissart's time, or the school of Dijon. Emile Mâle appears to me with his magnificent book *Religious Art in France, the Twelfth Century: A study of the Origins of Medieval Iconography. Et me voilà dans mes éléments* all I need is some Veuve Cliquot in the crystal glasses my father gave to my son William in Paris, to bring back to me in Melbourne in a paper bag (William wanted to leave these in each airport), and my drawing paper and good pens, in search of images to draw and explore and then transform into a painting. The impact of Christian art, ninth and tenth centuries, is great on me, seeing it as a child. I will probably interrupt myself and read Tolstoy or Dostoevsky, an essay in contrast by George Steiner, and train my brain to think a little, then grab André Malraux's *Le Monde chrétien*, a book of sculptures and tympanum, finding on page 78 the twelfth-century drawing *Vigneron dans sa Cuvé Médaillon du Tympan d'Autun*. I will go into ecstasy and draw to my heart's delight and desire. Sometimes I look at Flavius Josephus' old stories and descriptions of ancient Roman times and the life of the Jews in antiquity.

I travel endlessly like an eagle over mountains and dive on a track that will develop my work. The road is long and there is no respite for the wicked and even less for the virtuous. (An old beggar told me these words one Sunday in Rankins Lane, where I was living.) My love of talking to beggars comes from talking to *clochards* in Paris as a child. They have the wisdom of true thinkers and are the conscience of Paris if you only listen to them. In Melbourne, too, beggars are our conscience.

Writing this book is sheer torture as it takes me away from my work, but writing about one's span of life is a must, as you realise how you have worked, loved, studied – survived on this dangerous earth and faced your mortality. My work has always made me very secure but one angst remains: I have had it since about twelve, when I realised that the earth travels on its orbit and the earth will fall somewhere. Now you can see, reader, that my knowledge of astronomy and physics is lamentable, pitiful. All the same, this thought happens before I fall asleep. I try not to think of it, but the pleasure of the unknown universe is irresistible as I see strange indigo blues before sleep comes and saves me through the night for another day. My work makes me besotted, like a woman in love with her children, with a lover, with life. No escape, even in the arms of one's sleep – *dormiens*, a beautiful Latin word full of connotations.

There is a story I love very much. I discovered it in *Journal d'Eugène Delacroix*. It is a day where yellow is dull and the great Delacroix is struggling. He decides to go to the Louvre and investigate yellow by other great masters. He orders a hansom cab. When it arrives the hansom cab, by some peculiar coincidence, is yellow. As Delacroix puts his foot on the step he notices that the shadow under the steps is violet. He cancels his trip to the Louvre, goes back to his magnificent atelier and has found the solution to his problem. I must add that Delacroix admired Michel-Eugène Chevreul. There is a photograph of the great French photographer Nadar and Chevreul sitting together. Nadar photographed Delacroix, and I think of my friend Antoine Fauchery who studied with Nadar photography. A little world on my desk of ghosts, and my imagination running wild.

An image of my childhood still travels with me and begs to be painted. It is a romantic, very large print, maybe three metres long by three-quarters of a metre high. The painting lived in a dark studio at Passy in Paris where my aunty and uncle lived. The image is so haunting. It is a river scene or a lake, lots of trees, white swans, lots of beautiful nymphs in white veils walking through the water at knee level amongst the swans; some nymphs are in a boat which is quite long and thin. All seem extremely happy and busy walking and sailing through the water. White, dark green, black are the colours. The nymphs are gracefully walking and those in the boat are sitting, also very gracefully. I perceived at age four, approximately, the coolness, the peace, the movement, the restrained palette. As a child I always said I would be a writer but I also loved painting and drawing. To me, painting and drawing are natural, I've done them for as long as I can remember.

I am very inspired by the image, but can only paint it when my brain has crystallised the memory into a painting, and there lies the mystery of a painting, in my case. As the painter I am, I cannot create what is in front of my nose, my eyes (*l'exactitude n'est pas la vérité* – Vuillard), but only what my brain has digested; that is, only once the image has been distilled, very much like grape juice into good wine. It is probably one of the laws of nature I love most.

That is also why I love rare dolls, for they have captured the ephemeral in childhood and become art: time arrested; love captured in poetry, music, prose, architecture, painting, memory, history, maybe great cooking. But I have to admit that the process of rendering art remains a mystery, as the brain has to deal with such diverse material and input in daily life to produce the magic, to crystallise what is to be captured in an image – a familiar image as Matisse would say, as Cézanne would say – images that are simple and dormant in our ancient brains, where a serpent's brain still is.

Like the image of angels. When I was asked where it comes from I thought very deeply and remembered a fear of eagles as a child in France. The fear came from stories told of mothers going to the fields, *les glaneuses*, toiling the soil and leaving their young babies in the *langes*, swaddling, on the ground, and the *aigles* coming to get the babies from high in the sky. The *langes* and the wings of the eagle taking away the child. The horror could have created an image of a flying child, an angel, to soothe the pain. This is how I think. One needs time to study and clarify various 'primitive' ideas. One is, as I regard myself, a 'tool' of nature.

Once I was trimming a tree whose branches were mingling into another tree – my nectarine tree. I tripped over a ladder lying at the base of the tree I was trimming rather vigorously and I fell down. My first reaction was to think that the tree was punishing me for cutting its branches. My cat was all around me in a great state as I got up. I thought of the drawings of Arthur Rackham's trees. I thought of all the tales of people turning into trees. That little incident caused a vast tumult in my brain and somehow, if I am lucky, a tree painting could emerge.

These are two little examples of the birth of ideas that crystallise into paintings. It might take years or come soon. Being a painter is a little like being an athlete: you must take care of the body and mind so it can function well and be clear at all times to be receptive to images that may appear freely, unexpectedly. This is my way of working. Other painters have other ways. Mine is slow but sure and remains wondrous, and sad because life is so short. Also, I realise, my thinking is very simple and logic is not my forte. I read fine writing on theories of art and often it amuses me, and I remain as puzzled as ever and happy as I can be with my good paints and brushes.

But if I distil my thoughts, it is memory that surfaces and holds keys to our sanity, and haunts our lives, and is a potent force to enrich them and clarify many a foggy blockage in our minds. I think paintings help us to find our way in the crevasses of our brain: our brain is a lost city where a little lane might suddenly at its end reveal a large building with a sense of place where memory can bloom. Memory helps all the arts to enlighten us and us to engage with life head on, and joyfully, and to sort out many a troubling event and destruction. I see memory suddenly as a tree with many, many branches, and this is why trees stare at us and at the sky.

Siamese Twins, 1961

ABOVE *Bird With Brood*, 1958

OPPOSITE *Couple With Bird*, 1958

ABOVE *Little Boy With Bird*, 1964

OPPOSITE *Bird Embraced*, 1967

mirka 67

MIRKA 69

OPPOSITE *Koala*, 1973

ABOVE *Faun With Bird*, 1969

Angel With Dog, 1984

MY MEN

ome time before the death of Georges Mora, perhaps a month, I realised he was dying and a terrible pain set itself on the left side of my brain, above my ear – acute, like the knock of a giant's foot on my brain. It stayed four years and sometimes reappears if I fret, but rarely. It is fading away.

Georges always said I could have adventures with other men, but I was not to be too serious and must be home for dinner at 6.30pm. Two or three months should do of gallivanting, he thought. *Hélas*, my few affairs lasted longer – one for two years, one for eleven, and one for thirty-one years. I also explored three quickies, one out of sheer despair and ignorance, before my next two long liaisons. The affair with Georges never ended and lasted fifty-one years.

During the war in Paris, from 1940 on, my little friends disappeared one by one. One friend, Oliver, died at sixteen of a mysterious disease. He lived on the second floor below mine and we used to exchange letters, attached to a thread, down from my window to his, for two years at least. One day his mother found all the letters under his mattress. I was asked for the first time inside Oliver's home. There was a powerful grandmother sitting on a large bed with a big fur all over; she was reading the Bible and telling me she had married an English man. Then Oliver's mother, Madame Fourmansky, told me she had married a Russian man. All very confusing. They were both French ladies. Madame Fourmansky promptly came to the puppy-love notes and asked me to be less serious and told me how young I was to think so old, and to stop altogether writing to her son. She had two beautiful daughters, older than Oliver, who were dancers at the Casino de Paris. Sometimes the girls would take me with them to the Casino de Paris to watch them rehearsing. One had won a Shirley Temple competition in Nice when younger.

I gave back to Oliver the present he had given me, a *médaillon* on a chain with his photograph inside. He died a week later; for years I thought he had died because I returned the *médaillon*. I had been to the hospital to see him when I gave him back the *médaillon*; he was so white, and so thin, a shadow of himself. Oliver had also given me his grandmother's little Bible, which I still have and read sometimes. I only got a kiss from Oliver on my forehead. I carry his quality forever, we were both sixteen.

Once, around the same time, I was leaving a ball when a young man stopped me and wanted to take me to his room. I looked at his moustache above his lips, long and thin; the moustache was a sign of danger I thought and escaped home safely.

When we were hiding in the country during the war, I had images of the forest full of young boys and young girls, all fighters in the Resistance. In the village where we hid I never saw teenagers my age until they appeared one evening in springtime with lilac, and disappeared again – a ritual. At Saint-Quay-Portrieux there was François in the tree outside my bedroom. By then, I had read great love novels: *Amok* by Stefan Zweig, Colette's *Chéri*, all sorts of romantic works, Stendhal's *De l'Amour*, Napoléon's love letters to Joséphine. Ovid's 'How to Cure Yourself from Love', a poem. 'Penelope' in Homer's *Odyssey*. Not having had myself any real sex, I did not know what it was all about, but of course I thought I did.

In the eighties the professor Rene Thom came to Melbourne to give a seminar on the theory of chaos at Melbourne University and he spoke to me later. As I was showing him my drawing book, the professor became very interested and told me what my work was about: prey and predator. Did I get a surprise, as I regard myself *l'innocence en personne*.

I started to think about my various but few adventures with myself as prey, and in turn as predator. It is true that I prefer to chase a man rather than be chased by him. So, Mirka the predator. But once you catch your prey, as nature would have it, the predator becomes the prey. These views made me see my liaisons as very puzzling, and even more clearly. Being penetrated makes you a prey automatically – and you're a predator if you say yes too often. And what about pure love, as my husband Georges called my third liaison? I was the predator: I chased more than I was chased.

The second liaison I was a prey, as my sexual education started then, but I didn't know how good it was as it shaped itself. I understood it fourteen years later when I could compare it with different styles of sex making. That good teacher was Dr Allan Wynn, who eventually told my husband that he wanted to marry me. Georges just said, 'Mirka must choose.' As I already had one husband, I could not see the point of having another one, in my simple mind.

Years later, I was at a dinner party of people of a certain age. All the men knew Dr Allan Wynn and spoke of him, of all his humanitarian qualities, and how he fought for human rights. Then I heard a man say, 'But Allan Wynn was a womaniser.' My heart sank, even though it was a long time ago, the liaison with me, buried in time.

Georges, being a man of the world, understood the affairs of women. I was a child when we met and married. I am still learning, still dreaming of true love even though I am not too sure what it is, but I have seen it in action. I had married a bachelor, chased him for a year in Paris, and wanted a child, to be complete. I succeeded. Soon I found out that my husband lived in another world beside my own, beside our world – it is life.

In the early days of our marriage, Georges would say to me as he went to work in the morning, 'Some husbands never come back when they say goodbye.' After breakfast, Georges would smoke a Camel cigarette and its aroma would arouse me no end, but it was *peine perdue*, as Georges somehow didn't notice or had to go. Lots of good sex after breakfast lost forever.

Georges suffered terribly in his sleep at the slightest noise or movement by me, thinking the Gestapo was coming to get him, as had happened during the war. He was rescued by the Resistance. He was a very bad sleeper and soon we had to have our own bed sheets and blankets, and later we had separate beds. I was dumbfounded. Also, being a young girl and eager to discover all about my body and that of my husband, I was soon to be restrained, for good measure perhaps.

Nevertheless, Georges was and still is the pillar of my security, even in his grave. Nothing bad could happen to me as he always stood by me, understood everything, but he had to remain a bachelor. This I understood pretty quickly as Georges travelled a lot as soon as we were married. While he was away, I worshipped his photograph and did paintings and went to art galleries.

When we were still in Paris, Georges worked with inventors, not unlike painters in temperament. Before his trips he would ask R.B., one inventor, to take me out while he was away. The inventor looked a little like a young John Perceval, utterly delicious. Sexy. Dangerous. Muscular.

After a dinner with good wine, outside my apartment in rue Eugène Carrière I was in the car of R.B. and the young man asked me to hold his superb erect *fascinum*, or *balayette infernale* as you say in French argot. (*Pratique érotique imaginaire*.) I took it in my hand, crying, madly calling, '*Mouchi, Mouchi*', which was the nickname I gave my husband. Poor R.B. realised I was a hopeless case and let me go home. No instruction for me that time, just a lesson in incoherency and something nice in my hand.

As my husband was working with R.B., the young man would come to our apartment and I would giggle like an idiot girl, ready to be a prey for the next expert predator, who was to be Dr Allan Wynn, besotted with me, catching me when and wherever he could for all to see, giving me a great birthday party for my twenty-fifth, for all Melbourne's quality people. Professor 'Pansy' Wright stands in my memory, looking at me, and what a face he had, and wit and joyfulness.

After two years of frenzy, Allan realised I would not marry him and said we had to stop the wild closeness. What his *fascinum* could not do his hands did; and on my mouth, burning kisses galore. Dr Allan Wynn once organised a dinner at Florentino for

Dr Ainslie Meares, whom Allan had gone to see to try and free himself from his obsession with me. Dr Ainslie Meares said to Allan as I was being described to him but no name given, 'Oh, I am slowly falling in love with that person myself.' At the dinner, I was to sit on the right side of Dr Meares. Mrs Meares was there, Allan and Sally Wynn were there. It was a dinner party where my eyes were only on Mrs Meares and I didn't get one smile from her. Out of the five people present Mrs Meares had the strongest presence.

One day, I saw Allan on the other side of Collins Street opposite my studio, walking with another girl who was as pretty as I was, and I understood it was all over and I fainted on my doorstep, outside 9 Collins Street. Embarrassing.

As the years went by, everyone could see that Allan Wynn was longing for me still. He also wrote me letters of praise for my art. When he died, I was very, very sad; part of my youth, ignorant as it was, was going with his death. I left my home and walked for hours, crying, and walked and walked to nowhere.

After these two beautiful men, Georges and Allan, I became what I thought was an experienced woman. *Hélas*, far from it. Once I found myself in the back seat of a car having a long *fascinum* entering my body, and it was agreeable but I had no recollection of how I could have been lured into the back seat. He was seductive and good with words.

Another time, I was upstairs at the Mirka Café when a door opened and that same man from the car got me again and then I was not a prey any more. I turned into a predator to plan my next attacks – only two, mind you, but I was very competent by then. One was a charming man who played billiards, I had watched him right through the afternoon at some friends' place on a Sunday. The billiard balls falling in the net looked like live testicles, so arousing.

The young man was my prey, just once. That evening we made love classically, and later he married a French woman.

Another time, and the last time for this kind of exercise, was a man who came to collect me at the hotel where I was staying to go to some friends for dinner. I received him stark naked, lying on my bed. Though he was surprised and older than me, he jumped into bed, another prey, his hair was like silk and he was lucky.

These flings were like glasses of champagne, and though the acts were a folly *à deux*, I could see no meaning in them, just part of my education. I thought I was really learning well.

The third love affair was to be a great love. I was definitely the predator, I forgot the game and found myself many times a prey. More than the body, which was slightly effeminate, I loved the presence of the man. He understood paint and I could learn from him and develop my work. Georges spoke to him many times as I was getting too involved, which was not the rule my husband had established. I knew the rules of love, I was well versed in *De l'Amour* by Stendhal and also in the letters of Flaubert to Louise Colet. My affair with this man made everyone sad, as I had a little family and a husband I could not leave – or my husband would not let me go, yet.

This love affair ended, like all love affairs do, but better than most. With it, I could compare the prowess of my lovers and I didn't seem to improve in erotic knowledge, I needed to explore more. Writers are better than painters in bed, I read somewhere. With all my reading and the little experience I had, I definitely lacked interest in penetration; most of the time I preferred a real glass of champagne.

Somehow, being a married woman, even if you strayed, one's honour was always protected. This was old-fashioned thinking and I longed to be free one day and do as I pleased, to fend for myself.

These wishes happen anyway as your children grow and leave home and your husband also goes, sad as it is. Often when I see little old couples walking in the street, I wonder at it, as I always knew I would be alone one day and not know this life *à deux*, when you are old and walk arm in arm along the sea.

When I was young, I wanted to make love right through the night but Georges said it was not possible, so one day I eloped with my lover to Portarlington and stayed in an old mill house and made love right through the night. It *was* possible, but the cap I was wearing let escape a terrible smell in the morning. As it was an old mill, there was no hot water. The cold shower soon sobered me up but I still loved the night and being a predator, knowingly at that.

Back in Melbourne, John Reed asked me if I had seen the sensational lights of the Geelong Electric Plant. 'No, John,' I said, 'I was busy doing something else.' We both laughed.

My husband was distancing himself from me. I wish I had used my persistence on my husband, whose *robinet d'amour* (argot) was best of all. Still I respected his way of being towards me, his freedom, and though I was sad I went along with my life, near his life. I would have loved to resume a normal marriage, if this exists, but Georges refused, and our marriage, as it was, continued to survive: a little boat on the high seas but with a most safe anchor. Maybe there was nothing more to learn about sex, erotic books of photographs could give you all the eroticism you needed, when you needed it. I am lying through my teeth; nothing is as good as a good partnership, but nothing lasts but memories and it is good to have many if you can.

Being a painter you have the luck to orgasm as you paint, when the colours work well with each other, like the simultaneous contrasts of Michel-Eugène Chevreul. Lucky me, I have done a lot of painting, and as men slowly lose their mysterious powers, as one matures like a good wine, one considers deeply the past years and the progress of one's personality, and desire for the *fascinum* or *la vipère broussailleuse* (*membre viril* in good French argot) fades eventually. The brain is where pleasures are made, and brilliant men often are good with other tools besides their *fascinum*. They can say words and describe all sorts of things that transport you and give you pleasurable, incomprehensible orgasms. But don't tell them about it.

I think sex is a kind of drug like all other drugs, and to confuse love with sex is a great error, but they go nicely together. All ends in full circle, and once a virgin, as in my case, always a virgin. But woman is fickle and love is always around the corner, if one has the courage to be interested, engage. Make the world go round. I don't think I have yet, not for want of trying, but the interest is not wild enough; the learning seems to be a repeat and therefore not entrancing enough. *Et pourtant* I dream of a beautiful man who will know my slightest wishes, and I his, and share equally our tendernesses. But one is alone and it is bad to be a prey or a predator, even though it is the law of nature, who is not to be trusted – it kills.

As well as the three quickies, I did a *clarinette baveuse* to a man who needed it badly. He was a Jewish man and as I saw the immeasurable pain on his face, I could not refuse. He had a perfumed handkerchief and gave it to me to put his semen in – I had it in my mouth. An insane moment, event. He later offered to take me to orgies, but I always declined. He also offered to do the same to me later, but I always declined. His phone calls disappeared in time.

It reminds me of *The Grapes of Wrath* by John Steinbeck – *Les Raisins de la colère* – when a man who is dying is asking a woman with milk in her breast to feed him, and she does.

Strange, these encounters one has through one's life, searching for a good companion or passing the time.

Once, as I embraced a beautiful male friend who just came out of a swimming pool and who embraced me, I, who always wished to be a woman, was no sooner holding the large back of the man in my arms than, instead of feeling womanly, my brain tricked me and this big healthy back turned into my father's back and myself into a child at once, as my father often took me to swimming pools in Paris as a child. I was very disappointed with myself and yet as usual puzzled by what had just happened to my memory, active as it was, good at attention and often leading me astray.

Albert Camus said, 'There is an honour in love – once this is lost, love is nothing.' The honour of loving another being remains great in my mind, and now, past seventy, going towards eighty, I have much to learn still, in a hurry . . .

I am laughing to myself.

When I was nearing forty years of age, I decided to love a man in real life, as I had been conducting a love with the photograph of an old man in my book *Australia Unlimited* for three years. When I showed the picture to the young man I had set my heart on he said, 'That's my great-great-grandfather.' This is what I like in life, strange coincidences like this.

He was my fourth big love and had a possessive mother and a good *fascinum*. I chose of course, the most complex man, the most learned, and he had the same glint in his eye as the old man in the photograph. It was to be a long journey, not unlike Psyche and Eros in the fairy tales of Apuleius. Often a tale can guide you in real life but it is hard to decipher metaphors within metaphors, yet this is how our thinking goes, or mine does anyway: *la lumière de l'esprit* is a metaphor. My *amour* had a lovely sister who always took my phone call, but the mother didn't, or if she did she would say, 'What is wrong with you?' and hang up the phone. It took her twelve years to talk to me and twenty-five years, when she was on her death bed, to thank me for being so nice to her son. I miss her.

I met this man, my fourth love, when my husband Georges read an article on art in the *Nation*. Thinking it was an old man who wrote it, and liking the article very much, he invited the writer to come for dinner at Tolarno. The old man was actually a very young man of twenty-four, and I turned into a predator who soon was a most fragile prey. I am a slow learner.

Six months passed and the young man said, 'I want to go to bed with you.' I promptly said that it would have to be in another city, maybe Sydney as I was to have a show at Frank Watters' Gallery, the Erichthonius series, and I would be staying at the Belvedere, an idyllic place for such a tryst.

On my arrival in Sydney, that very night, on the same floor of the hotel the two next bedrooms were occupied by Al Alvarez and Charles Blackman respectively. Both men wanted to catch me, but I knew about doors that open and shut quickly by then.

The first night with a new lover is not always a success as you think of your ex-lover and want to recapture old habits. I wonder why, and I remember reading something written by M. Esther Harding, a Jungian psychiatrist, that explains why you search for ghosts in a new lover.

I was out to learn about having the courage to really get involved with a man and be interested in sex perhaps; even so the young man said, 'Do not take advantage of me.' Dumbfounded again, but like a fish about to be hooked, I got caught. It seems that love always takes over, and kindness and thoughtfulness – all in all, learning to be a good human being, and this is the hardest to achieve.

Colin Bingham, in *The Affairs of Women*, quotes Thackeray as saying, 'It is best to love wisely no doubt, but to love foolishly is better than not to be able to love at all.' And in the same book, I find Ninon de Lenclos, 1620–1705, *femme de lettres, française, née à Paris,* who said, 'Love never dies of hunger but often of indigestion.' I like the images hiding in the words.

As you enter a new adventure you forget all the good resolutions and it is sink or swim. I may never learn to protect myself, and having no pride left will be a willing fool. That is how I thought nearing the age of forty. No regrets, just learning. But falling in love this time was the cause of my breakdown. I realised I was dealing with my lover's mother and not with the young man – my brain was cornered, a tragedy.

A breakdown is a terrible thing. One day I noticed that my black cat Napoléon didn't sleep on my bed any more, because I was dying, I thought. That day, I got out of my bed and was on the road to recovery after three weeks of mental pain in my beautiful bedroom with all my rare, beloved books and dolls, with my poor husband and children and friends and Dr Smyth coming to see me. All the time, my brain not functioning. My only real friends were the bottles of Château d'Yquem that I kept under my bed and my cat Napoléon and the Italian lady from the kitchen at Tolarno who said, 'I know why you cry,' as she brought me food.

Later, as I got better, I noticed I was putting on a little weight and every time a little breakdown would come, I would lose some weight. I realised that minute breakdowns were a good way to lose weight; as soon as I realised this I never experienced a breakdown again, just becoming nice and round with the breast size I always wanted, and hips *à la* Rembrandt as well.

Loving a man is a difficult project. I needed much consoling as *le coeur a ses raisons que la raison ne connaît pas*. I heard this saying all through my childhood as I loved listening to women talking about their men – my mother and my Aunt Mimi especially. My mother had chosen my uncle for her sister to marry and she felt responsible for their marriage troubles. After my aunt was taken by the Nazis to Drancy in Paris, her husband went in the street in his underpants, was arrested and taken to a madhouse, where he spent his days and nights right through the war. He was a professor of Esperanto. After the war, he called some other professors from the Sorbonne, who remembered him and rescued him.

As a child I did not like my uncle, though he always had books under his arms. I think I didn't like him as I knew he was giving my Aunt Mimi a hard time. He also had a way of looking at me that made me feel uneasy. I was seven or eight and peeling green beans. It was summer. In our home I could hear Mother talking in another room to someone and this made me feel secure. Another friend my mother had was called Madame Rosa and I loved listening to them talking about men. Madame Rosa wore her lipstick in a way I didn't like. It had on her top lip the shape of a heart. Her mouth was too small though. Men were villains, they said over and over again, especially the *coureur de jupons* – petticoat chasers.

When Madame Rosa and her husband Jeesky came to our house a kind of joyous mood invaded the house. Jeesky would give rides on his ankles to my sisters and me, we would also get some money to buy lollies. His dog bit my sister Salomèe on her leg slightly as she was climbing the stairs. Madame Rosa, who was very jealous, suicided and was found dead in a little pond, and for years I could not understand how she drowned in such little water. Altogether, I observed as a child that men were a cause of much trouble and yet fun was had as well. But the show must go on, and with touches of Bouvard and Pécuchet can only end in a poignant way. We always have to part, it is inexorable, and suddenly I remember a little song Paulette would sing to me:

Un poète m'a dit
qu'il était une étoile
où l'on s'aime toujours.

C'est l'étoile d'amour
c'est l'étoile du rêve
les amants, les maîtresses
s'aiment la nuit et le jour.

Well, with our space travels she might be right.

Many men desired me and I always said to them, 'If you still like me when we're seventy we shall see.' Two of them took fright as they reached seventy, and died. Others forgot but one did not, and passing his seventieth birthday he rang one day to ask if I would consider marrying him. It was my dearest friend John Perceval. His voice troubled me and his request honoured me but a painter can't really get married, even though one dreams of it, and there I am, incapable of saying no and incapable of saying yes.

MY CHiLDReN

 have drawn my children
and painted them endlessly and I cannot distinguish them from my
soul. They live there. Having children is an impossible great love
affair and no matter if the seas or mountains or a few streets separate them from you, they remain unattainable.

It starts with their first day at kindergarten. The parting is
unbearable. You come home and all of their lovely noises have disappeared but are present; toys, clothes, shoes are all silent but you
can hear and smell them. At the end of the day you will see the children again and real life will start again. It is so hard to be a parent
as we also have to grow, like our children. At a different pace but at
the same time.

I have kept lots of events that happened to my children in a
baby book. Every night before the children went to bed, I would
ask, 'Is there anything you would like me to write in the baby

book?' The book also included my own observations, and sometimes Philippe, William or Tiriel would add things – they always had access to the book. The last time Philippe visited me, in October 1999, he asked to see the baby book and was very pleased, being a filmmaker, to read that I had described him as resembling Orson Welles when he was only three months old.

The baby book is written in French and English. It covers the children's first delicious behaviour to achieve their wilful desires of all sorts, their learnings, their relationships to each other, their care, their friends. Endless achievements, endless normal anxieties, their girlfriends and boyfriends, their poetry, their poignant childhoods as they had to grow, and grow they did, faster than me.

Now I am alone with the baby book full of moments I have captured. The book also mirrors my life as a mother in the midst of always protecting my work, and as a woman in love trying to be a complete woman and trying to understand what that means. Perhaps it is to show your children what a person is first and a mother second. Tough aim, but it was my aim and I tried my best to achieve it, often to the consternation of those around me.

Soon, I discovered that my little children were little visitors passing by and equal to me. We all had to learn so much as we were growing. Once – I must have been in a kind of trance which lasted a millionth of a second – I could not understand why I was not a child at the same time as my children, same size as them. That gap between mother and child is always there. We travel together and then we have to part, and it is very sad but we can't be a tribe forever in our new society, we have to go and find new places where our potential can bloom and we have to part often. I think I need to read at once *Look, Listen, Read* by Claude Lévi-Strauss, which I have just bought. He talks about the place of art in human life; this rare man always calms me down and enriches me wherever I am, in whatever mind state I am in.

Talking or thinking about your children and grandchildren is very much like being in front of a large canvas, the best in the world with the most beautiful brushes and of course the best paint ever, and being in a state of grace. We aim at capturing a real painting, the soul. This life's quiverings.

My children somehow move in time, back and forward in my brain like art does. There are memories I always go back to, and as I grow older, the void which frightened me as a young girl is slowly full of minute and big events, the big events more and more related to past events that knitted themselves around my children. So, we are our children even as we fade away slowly like a beautiful love affair.

My eldest son Philippe is a filmmaker and painter. My second son William is an art dealer. My youngest son Tiriel is an actor, and all of my sons can draw and write beautifully. My grandchildren have good genes for love, for learning and writing, and I wish I could live forever to see all of my grandchildren grow. But this is the big dream, and we can 'see' ahead even if we have to go, dissolving into stars in the convenient universe and filling it with more stars. The idea of fractals (discovered along with their mathematical theory in 1975 by Benoît Mandelbrot) slowly enters my mind and I dare think that maybe we are meant to live forever and that this will happen, with the right genes.

The beautiful mothers of my grandchildren come with their various ancestors from near and far away. Lucy, Pamela and Freya: fractals placing themselves elegantly in their children's personalities. I think I am using the term 'fractals' as a metaphor yet again, as it is so difficult to catch the stuff we are made of, but I like the image of fractals. Delacroix was not unaware of it in his observations when painting trees.

From the baby book:

4TH MARCH 1968   *Vacances merveilleuses à Aspendale nous avions deux maisons et dans l'une les enfants jouaient à* Ned Kelly, guns, robbers, etc. Towards the end of the holidays the Percevals came to live in the empty house next door. The children had another kind of holiday: as many girls as boys. Winkie, the first day, gave a big thrashing to Peter G. because he attacked William, so he didn't come to our house for a while.

The children saw a bushfire on the beach, and a second one for which they were slightly accused. The next day Philippe was quite sick; at night when Philippe had to go to the toilet, he always wanted me to go with him. The boys went to the carnival once with the Gawiths. They also went to Mordialloc with the Perceval girls.

One day I gave Philippe and William some money to go with Peter and Tiriel to buy a little bike for Tiriel, which they did.

A NOTE FROM PHILIPPE TO ME   Can you press my pants for open day, they haven't been ironed since I bought them. Dress nicely for my open day. Comb Tiriel's hair and *make* him put his nice pants on. Put blue stockings on and put that greenish yellowish dress on – you know, the tight dress. The one you were wearing when you went to the doctor with *Mouchi*. Sleep well! Bibs.

A LETTER FROM TIRIEL TO HIS GRANDMA, MY MOTHER, AFTER I LEFT HOME   My dearest Grandma, I really appreciate the ten dollars you have so very nicely given me. I feel you have worried about me a bit too much. I am thirteen now and if I say so myself I am more mature now. I feel I can cope with what's happened and what's happening. I'm well taken care of and what has happened hasn't greatly affected my life, I'm still quite happy.

Everlasting love,

Tiriel xxxx xxx

29TH DECEMBER 1971, A LETTER FROM WILLIAM TO HIS FRENCH TEACHER   Punishment. Firstly, I do not think I was creating a disturbance which would hinder Madame West from teaching and I think I am being unduly punished. I think it is a pretty sad state of affairs when somebody is not allowed to laugh. But if Madame West thinks that this is a sin, I will try and refrain myself from laughing during your periods and I apologise *if* I was disturbing the teaching of your class which I think I was not. I would also try to point out that I come into your classes with the intention to work and I do work well, you say that yourself and I think it is unfair to pick on me just because you can't find the real culprits.

William Mora 3E

(Signed, Mirka Mora)

FROM TIRIEL, 20TH NOVEMBER 1975   Mum, I finished my exams today. I am going to Holbrook tomorrow. *Brother, Can You Spare a Dime?* has been nominated for an Oscar.

Love,

Tiriel

I think when I am long gone, my children will love their baby book, and lots of memories will bounce up for them out of my observations, always written in haste but captured.

I had lunch on the seaside at Donovans in 1997 with my grandson Rainer, who had just returned from a trip, quite long, in Europe. On his return he spent some time with his father, Philippe, in LA. He thought Pamela, Philippe's second wife, had been so nice to him, and to discover three half-siblings at once was also a joy. He asked me for their birthday dates. He is a scholar and very fine.

I spent time in Cannes in 1994 with Philippe and Pamela and their children Maddie, Georgie, Dominic. Our house was in Mougins, where Jack Thompson came one night bringing with him all I love about Australia: passion and fairness. I was sad at the Nice airport when I left my little family and I sobbed and sobbed in the aeroplane and through the corridors to the plane. It is very cruel to be parted from your family, even though one is a phone call away.

Tiriel went to live in Sydney, via England and the USA, where the film *The Castle* was launched. I waited for his return even before he left, and so it goes. Another merry-go-round.

In Melbourne I have William and Lucy's little family, with their children Lily and Freddie who give me great joy. Freddie shows great talent at drawing and painting. He thinks very well and loves my big teddy bears and small ones, who slowly go to live in his house and then come back to my house. At nine years of age, Lily won a Creative Arts Scholarship at Melbourne Girls Grammar School. Already she is a collector and has very rare fish that she takes great care of and a cat called Sushi. Lily is very sociable, and while she looks a lot like her mother, she also looks like me. She paints well and is a very studious thinker.

Lucy is a thoughtful daughter-in-law (*belle-fille*) and gave me a little cat, Pompom number 2, who I adore. When Lucy presented the kitten to me she looked very naughty as she didn't ask me if I wanted a cat. Needless to say, I am besotted with Pompom, who is three years old now and teaches me to clean my little house and feed myself. He has a shower with me and thinks he is a dog. When I write, he always sits on my chair and follows me from room to room – the painting room, the writing room, the kitchen, the garden, rain or shine. Pompom is a true friend. Everyone admires him, or is confused by his large size. I feed him well when I can and I suddenly remember a book by Colette, *Douze dialogues de bêtes*, that I found once in a second-hand book shop with an ex-libris of Dorothea Mackellar. The book was the French edition. It is a story about cats who witness the end of a love affair and describe all the nuances of the two people's behaviour – sad and funny. Cats are very observant.

Dominic, when he rings from LA, is very passionate and does not want to share his granny with anyone. This is the kind of man I love. Maddie writes very well, loves kittens, loves to describe the clothes she wears when I ask her to describe them, and is very pleased to have a Waterman fountain-pen I sent her. Georgie is also very pleased with a pen astronauts use in outer space. He is very fine and could be a great actor and writer. Maddie still wants to be an actress, she occupies a large space in my soul. She also wants to come and stay with me. Long ago, we used to watch *ET* together.

In April 1998 Freddie invites me to visit his new school. He is very affable and only six years old. It is family day at that lovely school. I could write about my family endlessly, but Pompom my cat calls and a guest is coming for dinner tonight, and it is time for a glass of Veuve Clicquot – a charming man gave me a bottle last week. Like the French writer Colette who had cats on her writing table, I am indulging my cat for the moment, purring, purring, both of us still on my chair, keeping me warm as it is cold today.

It's 14th July 1998, Republic Day for France. Deep in my heart, I miss the childhood of my children. I have not been able to lose my own childhood. The boys have grown into men and that's how it should be, even though I haven't got over having young children. I still buy prams and toys and play with toy cars, marbles – but the children have gone, I tell myself. All I can do is read Marcel Proust again and dissolve into the ether soon, but before that I still have some paintings to do, to soothe my funny brain, my greedy brain who wants my children back. Just as well I have the baby book to read and can relive many episodes that have gone so fast in my life as a mother.

20TH APRIL 1962   As I was promenading the other day with Tiriel in his little pusher on Collins Street, a very amusing incident occurred. Tiriel started to scream, 'A monster, a monster!' The monster was a very tall lady of a certain age wearing a hat that made her look as if she had horns. Straight away the poor lady put her hand on her hat while walking away, and turned her head several times to look at us fiercely.

21ST FEBRUARY 1969   Philippe has had great success in London. Two exhibitions; articles in *Nova*, *Art International*, *Art and Artists*. *Mouchi* went to see Philippe in London; he drinks vodka, smokes a lot, works sixteen hours a day. Prepares his film, *Trouble in Molopolis*. Tiriel does TV commercials and is a born actor. Very serious and draws excellently with black lead pencils.

9TH SEPTEMBER 1961   Philippe saw Tiriel crossing Collins Street and ran towards him. The tram came along and Tiriel fell head first into the oncoming tram. Philippe screamed and shouted, 'Shit!' Tiriel went underneath the tram and against the board protecting the wheels, which saved him. Philippe dived underneath the tram and brought out Tiriel. Philippe's version of the story ended with Mr Snow, the milkbar man, bringing them into the shop and giving Tiriel a bottle of Coca-Cola.

William's version: 'Ivor, a friend of ours, called Philippe, my brother, across the road. Me and Tiriel were on the other side of the road. Tiriel let go of my hand and I tried to get Tiriel, but a car came in front of me. I shut my eyes when I saw the tram coming and then I opened my eyes and saw a crowd of people around Tiriel and the tram. Our friend Mr Snow the milkbar man brought Philippe, Tiriel and me into his shop. He said, "Don't tell your mother because she is sick and it might make her much worse than she already is." So I said to her, "Philippe and Tiriel have gone for a walk." Then Tiriel came back with tears in his eyes and black all over his clothes, smelling of oil, and my mother said, "What has happened?" Our friend Ivor was here and he said, "Well, you see . . ."'

All this during one afternoon outside 9 Collins Street as I tried to rest inside.

22ND DECEMBER 1962   Philippe has finished a hard year of school work and come top of his form. He had a three-month

involvement with a girl called Golda. Long phone calls. She had
her appendix out and Philippe went every day at lunchtime to
see her, in hiding from her mother who didn't like the
relationship. Philippe ended it in a very mature way, enjoying
not being involved with the girl who took all his thoughts for
three months. My behaviour and approach to a lot of things –
the way I dress, the way I cook – seems to upset Philippe very
often up to tears and he pities me.

William jumped a grade and will go to the next year, all
this in the last two months. He has had an attack of pneumonia
and has had a hard time with Philippe and Tiriel. Philippe is
determined to be the chief. Tiriel has fits of temper and bites
everybody and throws things at other children but doesn't mean
it. Then lots of tears from everybody appear.

Mouchi had a terrible sickness in his foot and body, but is
well again. He is very touchy but very nice and the same
marvellous man he always has been, but our private life seems
very vulnerable and fragile. It has become an illusion,
untouchable. One lives along with it even though one's heart is
quiet, as if under an anaesthetic.

15TH SEPTEMBER 1961   I dreamt I was on a river boat on the
Seine, coming up the river. Suddenly my boat was walking on
wheels on the street opposite the Quai de la Tournelle in Paris.
I started to cry, 'Aspendale, Aspendale, I want to go home. What
am I doing in Paris?' My boat turned around a familiar corner,
entering a street. It was rue Maître Albert where I last lived as a
child with my parents and before my wedding. Next, I went up
the stairs into a building. I had William and Tiriel in my arms,
both babies. On one knee I had a big sore with pus running

away underneath the skin on each side and out onto my leg.
I entered a room and I saw legs covered with pants and a white
dressing gown looking like my husband's, and I looked up at the
body standing in front of me and I saw the two hands holding a
small black revolver aiming at me. Then I looked at the face of
that body and it was myself, well made up, shooting and trying
to kill myself. Then Tiriel woke up in the middle of the night
and woke me up. It was a blessing.

My little boy William has been drawing stick figures for the past
few days; very surprised, I watch the feet of the figures shrinking
until one day the feet have disappeared. I am intrigued as William
goes to Katy Gorham and Natacha Kirsta's ballet school once a
week. I ask William if he likes the ballet lessons. He says, 'No, I
don't like it any more.' So at once I cancel the ballet lessons and
I continue to watch my child's drawings of the stick figures. Every
day, the feet grow longer and I am very pleased with myself, to have
discovered my child's inner life through the succession of his drawings. It is 1959 in Melbourne.

The first outing in Paris with Philippe, in 1949, one hour in his
pram, I went into rue Veauvenargues, rue Damrémont, rue
Marcadet. I was a young mother pushing a little pram, wondering
what fate had in store for me and my baby. In Melbourne, in the
Fitzroy Gardens, I am pushing a large pram with Tiriel in it. I go
daily to the Fitzroy Gardens where I meet Maurice Chevalier and
we talk gently under the fig trees.

For William's first outing in his bassinet, we go by car to Kew
for afternoon tea at Gertie and Klaus's, who are new friends. It is
21st August 1953 and I am a mother and I know this is a time that

will disappear; I still have to do some growing up and my children are catching up with me.

15TH OCTOBER 1961   Philippe is doing tremendous assignments for school work. He is a hard worker. He went to the theatre yesterday with William and Simon Wynn, the play was *Oliver*; at night-time he went to Preshil, *une réunion des anciens élèves de Preshil*. He spent the night at the Anschels' and came home Sunday morning like a young man; he had to give the change from one pound that his father had given him yesterday. 'Shit, shit' is written in the baby book, as he has access to it always.

William has this week started to take his bike to the park and the first day could straight away ride it. William is very impatient sometimes. He dances beautifully and often dances for me on the big table to tunes on the radio. He always wants to go early to school where he helps the lady teacher. William brings interesting things to school and has to go from classroom to classroom to show his treasures: *une carapace de tortue*, and a tortoise's skull. He goes often to have lunch at the Balzac. William plays for hours with Tiriel at cowboy games.

Tiriel speaks more and more and is very impatient, very inquisitive, very charming. As soon as he works with paints, pencils, plasticine, or when he has a pencil in his hand, he calls it his homework, mimicking Philippe. He has a big vocabulary, 'sha up' for 'shut up', 'fuck you' and 'don't be funny'. He has recently discovered great joy to go by himself to buy milk, one orange, a little box of tubes of paint. He calls William his William, Philippe his Philippe, *Mouchi* my daddy, and me

Mum. Tiriel loves lollies, chocolate and eats very little else. He refuses meat and fish. He loves to prepare his own chocolate. Tiriel is cuddly and loves *papouillettes* – little bits of soft wool.

There we were living in Collins Street, next to Hearns Hobby, the toy shop, the milkbar and the fruit shop and the Fitzroy Gardens; what adventures for my little boys living in the city, and also for our two cats who kept being locked up in the doctor's room. We had to call the police to get our cats back as they would otherwise be meowing all night in the locked doctor's room at the back of the studio in the lane. The newsreels were another attraction at all the cinemas. Often the children would add to or correct my comments in the baby book. Philippe wrote, at about the age of thirteen, 'I don't approve of her bloody beer drinking' (which I would do with Perceval).

6TH JUNE 1962   William went riding on a horse with the Perceval girls and it was thrilling when he came home *ses yeux brillaient de joie*. Philippe didn't go because he doesn't like to hurt animals. The first Sunday of August 1958, John and Sunday took William and Philippe to Geelong to visit Sweeney, who was at Geelong Grammar School for a short time. Philippe was describing me the day and Sunday Reed. 'She is beautiful, she is like a dream, she is like God.' At nine years old, Philippe was really charmed by Sunday. I was very impressed. He draws very extraordinary drawings and the last few days he is preoccupied by landscapes. Philippe can read very well and devours books. He is fascinated by running writing as until now he only wrote in printing letters.

16TH JUNE 1974, A POEM BY TIRIEL

All his life,
nothing he'd done
was right
an' everybody said it
an' he couldn't take it any . . .
. . . longer

                                   A
                             F
                        F
                    O
                P
              M
           U
so he decided to J
                             C
                             L
                             I
                             F
                             F

you see he thought that that was
the only thing he would do right
but as he was F
            A
              L
                L
                  I
                    N
                      G

he thought that what he'd done
was wrong
that was the last thought he had
an' it was right.

6TH JUNE 1962 (BY WILLIAM)   Bibiche [Philippe's pet name]
wanted me to sleep with him and Tiriel for the night so we
would be warm. Bibiche is a serious boy.

26TH AUGUST 1969   William went to Sydney to do chores for
Mouchi. Pick up the Picassos – cheques at Clune.

17TH NOVEMBER 1958   Tiriel was overdue two weeks and
came very easily into the world. He tumbled out and I sat down
and looked at him; he was fresh like a rose. Tiriel seemed to
focus as soon as he was born, smiled a lot at one week old. Had
his first afternoon out at Gertie's terrace in Kew at two weeks,
and the next days under an orange blossom tree at Sunday and
John's place at Heide.

21ST MAY 1960   *William a toujours son charme extraordinaire et
a l'air d'avoir besoin de beaucoup d'affection. Il bouge sans arrêt
comme un petit poisson. Il a eu récemment une paire de chaussures
en daim qu'il adore absolument.*

Charles Blackman came this afternoon and lay down on
the floor to show us a drunk man; five minutes later, Tiriel did
the same thing. We all applauded him, and without moving *il a
souri aux anges*. He is a born actor.

Philippe and William are very taken by the hit parade.
They went yesterday to a lunch session to listen to Johnny
Devlin, and William was almost squashed by the people and
started boxing all around him at random and got some space.

23RD NOVEMBER 1960   William went to the Balzac for lunch,
saw *Mouchi*, then went to the men's toilet upstairs at 1.20 and

got locked up till 3 o'clock. A customer came and heard William screaming and then went down and got help, and then a waitress undid the lock. William first cried then stopped, called, 'Help! Help!' for about an hour, then said, '*Mouchi, Mouchi,*' sat down on the floor, stood on the toilet lid and shouted through the window. The waitress put William in a taxi and I waited for William at 9 Collins Street.

It was just the day of the last examination of the year for William [added by Philippe]. Some days later Mirka went to the school and told the teachers why William missed his exams. The teacher said he could go on to the next grade.

21ST MAY 1960   Philippe had four parts in a play: a robber, a cannibal, a witness, and himself in his classroom. He is crazy about films and can never see enough. He is a hard worker without respite and loves to collect all sorts of things: books, aeroplanes to build, stamps.

5TH MAY 1964   Saw Nureyev last night, very charming and delicate and adored by the muses. The children loved the ballet and we giggled every time Nureyev jumped and his tight costume showed his goodies. Eventually, all the rows of people laughed also.

2ND SEPTEMBER 1960   Philippe washed his jumper and that of William and hung them in the drying cabinet.

21ST AUGUST 1958   Philippe has lost one of his best friends at school. The child fell at school while playing with Simon and Philippe and fractured his skull and died the same day in his home. This has given a terrible shock to Philippe and has made him more profound and he suffers in silence. Philippe walked home with his friend and together would buy lollies and comics. The boy has been buried today. Last night Philippe was crying in his bed *à chaudes larmes* and I had to give him, or rather *Mouchi* gave him, an Aspro and he fell asleep.

During that time William very loudly said, 'I am trying to cry too but I can't make myself cry.' William is absolutely a model child, like a dream. He has a rich personality, an extraordinary ease with words, an irresistible charm. *Tous ses mouvements sont la grâce personnifiée*. There is a woman who wants to buy William and William thinks this is ridiculous and she should buy a doll, because dolls are for people who have no children. *Pensée plutôt profonde*.

Presently, I am reading *The Life of the Bee* by Maurice Maeterlinck and from time to time I tell the children some details and the children are very impressed and William retains each sentence. The great joy of Philippe is drawing with me, that is to say that I draw and Philippe adds details, often very important – to the great joy of William who each time observes us avidly. The children have much affection for the expected baby. Recently they have developed the habit of sleeping with something woolly under their head.

Ils ont chacun de ce fait un châle fait de laine fine. Simon has spent the afternoon with Philippe and when they parted Philippe had his eyes full of tears and was trying to hide them. I pretended not to see, even though his face was so distressed. Afterwards he drew a skeleton in a chest box and wanted to write the name of D. but he didn't succeed, therefore he scribbled on the name half written and then did a drawing who seemed to be a winged skeleton which suddenly gave him shivers of fear. Tonight he read for a long time *Adventure on Keri Island*. He read a long part of the book in William's new bed. William is absolutely crazy about his new bed and asks everybody to come upstairs to see his new bed, who is a little higher and bounces, to the great joy of William.

William, tonight as he slowly went to sleep, couldn't stop saying, 'I am so happy, I am so happy.' During the day he needed to swear and I told him he could say any 'rude' things to me as I love him so much and it would not matter if he addressed himself to me to swear. William dreams of a car with a big bell like that of the firemen. Philippe dreams of a telescope and, especially, both boys dream of a television. I hope to sell a painting one of these days to satisfy these dreams.

MY WORKSHOPS

he workshops I have con-
ducted consisted of painted dolls or soft sculptures, plaster dolls,
embroidery, masks, talking, writing, drawing, painting, mixed
media, and so on. My workshops would fill up books. I have conducted so many in Australia, also in France, in Connecticut, USA,
and in Yokohama in Japan, where Antoine Fauchery was buried in
1861 at only thirty-seven years old, and I didn't remember to find
his grave in my excitement.

Once, in a taxi on a rainy day, late afternoon, I was on my way
to conduct a workshop in Wodonga. As we passed a cemetery I
remembered that the body of Mad Dog Morgan was buried there in
an unmarked grave. The driver knew the story of Mad Dog
Morgan the bushranger and where the grave was. We stopped and
in the rain, on my knees, I rested near the body – I think the
cranium was in London. Last century, in Australia, bushrangers

were thought to be abnormal and their brains were studied in London – Mad Dog Morgan's testicles were made into a tobacco pouch. My son Philippe made a rare film about Mad Dog Morgan, whose story was written by Margaret Carnegie. The film was shown in Cannes, representing Australia in 1978.

In Brisbane in the early seventies, Ainslie Gotto's mother Leslie organised a one-week workshop for me. She did it with style. This was one of my first and I stayed in a good hotel and received a good fee. It was a large workshop, with children and adults mixed. One little boy didn't want to go back to school after a week with me and kept saying, 'I want to go to Mirka's school.' Later, at a workshop I did at the Royal Melbourne Institute of Technology, I held the class outside the lift, so I could catch people who normally wouldn't come. There, for a week, a fabulous woman who was a scientist came every day, just ten minutes, and achieved a lovely face, painted clay under cloth, on a stick.

Many workshops over a period of twenty-three years were done at the CAE. Reminiscing about their childhood and adolescence had a remarkable impact on the students and me, and we knew each other a little bit closer as the classes lasted for ten sessions each. Again we had all ages. One young mother came with a terrible problem: her little boy of two years old refused to pee in the toilet, he only liked to pee in the dining room. I could see that at each class the young mother was very troubled. We all got involved with what to do, many ideas were proposed, but to no avail. I thought about what I would do if it was my child and I suggested to the young mother to buy two potties and use them in the bathroom at the same time – that is, the mother uses one potty, the boy uses the other potty – and it worked. The child resumed going to the bathroom and not the dining room.

In another class, reminiscing about adolescence was to be extremely devastating, but thankfully each student stood their ground carefully and I monitored the perilous situation bravely. One lady, as a teenager, had been in Auschwitz concentration camp and she described the long march out of the camp, for miles, as the Russians were coming close to the camp and the Germans tried to take the people from the camp with them. There was another lady in that class, a German woman, blonde, who brought photographs taken during the Second World War of herself with a lioness sitting on a bench, and some photos had also German soldiers in their uniforms. She was oblivious of the situation, or had closed her mind. This is a class I will never forget; the students took care of each other very humanely.

At the same class was a very remarkable Australian woman from humble origins who was in her seventies. I would use a word to start the reminiscing and it would open many doors. Tears and laughter. For that lady I chose the word 'apple'. She remembered being in a school playground in a little country town during a very hot summer. I can just feel the hot sun. She had saved pennies for days to buy an apple. As she had the apple in her hand, her father passed the playground on a cart pulled by a horse; she offered her apple to the father, who took it.

Recalling the story, the lady realised that she had always sacrificed herself for everybody in her family. It was a revelation for her. The next week she returned to our class and told us that she had enrolled at the university to study. She changed her life. When I met her again as she was nearing eighty years old, she was a brilliant and secure woman. What an apple can do! Garden of Eden, eat your heart out. It reminds me of a story about the Garden of Eden that my son William brought back from the outback. The story was that if Adam had been an Aboriginal man, he would have eaten the snake. And all the world would be better, methinks.

During another session at the same workshop, I picked the word 'snake' and someone had a story for it. Again, it was in a little country town in Australia, again the children were playing in the schoolyard, when a snake appeared, quite large and black. The teacher, who was a man, called the firemen to come and pick up the snake, and by doing that he lost his job as the people in the village thought the teacher was a coward for not dealing with the snake himself. Another snake story was that of a young farm-help girl who, after a long day's work, went to bed and turned over her pillow to discover that a nice snake had found his sleeping place there. My story was of walking with friends after a nice lunch in Beauvais in a forest full of *cèpes* and lilies of the valley. I was left behind, as I usually walk slowly, when a lovely green viper crossed my path. It was so pretty, I didn't have time to be afraid. I was in utter wonder and never forgot its light-green/yellowish colour.

In these workshops I thought I should share my knowledge with the students and I always had great success with their achievements, except two or three times through the years when some students didn't grasp my way of inviting them to great creative adventures. It is very hard to give workshops when you are a painter: a one-day workshop costs a week of your time as you think of your students and their work for days after the workshops. You also have to gear yourself days before as well and readjust for days later. After many years with the CAE I was very honoured to be the recipient of the Sir Zelman Cowen medal and to be identified as an outstanding contributor to adult education, a field in which Sir Zelman himself has few peers. I remember giving another workshop in a school in Brisbane when Sir Zelman was the

Dean of the University of Queensland. Sir Zelman came one day to invite me to his family home and have breakfast, to meet his children and beautiful wife. I was very moved and honoured.

A workshop in France, which took two years to organise, was called Adventure in Art: Mirka en Provence. John and Shirley Traynor were the tour leaders. This was a workshop I could not refuse; I had not returned to France for as many as forty years. My husband Georges had just died and I didn't know then that I already had advanced cancer in my womb.

We flew straight to Paris with twenty-seven lovely students, males and females. The itinerary was not organised by me – for some reason, I had said no. Of course it included almost all the places I had been with my husband. We had a large bus and the driver didn't speak English. When the first interpreter we had – a charming girl I teased – had to leave, I took over and learned a lot of new words about the highways and names of trees I had forgotten: the highways drank the rain and were not slippery. The first night, on the avenue de l'Opéra as I walked with the Traynors, I saw a little French doll slipping out of the window of an antique shop. All my bankcard credit disappeared, but what joy to be in Paris with a doll.

The last night in Paris, Jenny, a lady who became my very dearest friend, insisted that I should come with her friend out for dinner, so Jenny, Sonia and I went out to the Brasserie Lip before going home to Australia. Our waiter was from Sydney and quite nostalgic for Australia. I was also looking for a book I had seen in Arles, by Federico Zeri: *Behind the Image: The Art of Reading Paintings*. The bookshop was called Le Divan and it was opposite the Église St-Germain-des-Prés and near Les Deux Magots, the café where Sartre and De Beauvoir went so often to write.

As I was so sick, we couldn't spend all night out and had to go back to the hotel, and next morning we left to catch an early plane to go home to Melbourne. *C'était un voyage bouleversant.* In the place du Tertre a waiter was lusting after a watercolour of two lit-tle lovers I was working on. I gave it to him and now my drawing is living with a real waiter in Montmartre where he lives, maybe as a lover, in a little Emile Zola room, like in his novels. There is another book to write about that trip and my friend Jenny, a painter and a writer, has written a good, unpublished recollection of it.

When I went to see my mother in 1980, the Connecticut University invited me to conduct a workshop. A good painter I had met organised it and I was much honoured. The position was called contact-artist, the equivalent of artist-in-residence. The painting studio was gigantic, I could not see inside the students' eyes. I asked them to bring their desks closer to me so I could see their eyes. I think we made painted dolls, which I call soft sculptures, and talked a lot.

One beautiful young woman came toward me during the day to question me. She had the smallest waist I had ever seen, she was quite forceful, and her question was, 'Can you have children and paint as well?'

'Yes,' I said, 'but you have to be well organised.'

'I'm glad,' she said, 'I have five children.'

'Just as well,' I said, 'you can have children.'

In the early nineties Melbourne Port and Yokohama Port organised an artist-in-residence exchange. I was happy to say yes and to have Kate Durham as my assistant, plus three interpreters. We had fifty students, ten days of solid work; we made painted dolls and plaster dolls. It was a great success. A student of a certain age who could speak English said to me, 'You are really teaching us freedom.' This was my greatest reward, as when students often ask, 'What do I do now?', I regularly answer, 'What would you like to do?'

One night, I decided to go for a walk in the Chinese quarter all by myself; I wanted to test my memory and find my way back to the hotel alone. During my little walk, I sat down on a bench to look at a black cat without a tail. I called, 'Puss, puss,' made noises with my mouth; the cat didn't take any notice of me. I learned later from an exquisite Japanese man at a dinner in Melbourne that I should have said, 'Cat-o, cat-o,' and the cat would have come to me at once. To say thank you, I told him I saw pigeons in Yokohama which seemed larger than ours. He was very pleased. Do pigeons eat cats? I wondered, thinking of the missing tail. I called the conversation *sans queue ni tête* and we all laughed.

When visiting the doll museum, where I saw lifesize dolls of children capturing the poignancy of childhood, the thought of Hiroshima invaded my soul – I cried. The dolls were staring at me. These were dolls the emperor would offer as a present to guests when they came to stay in the palace, circa 1880.

In Yokohama I made a lovely friend in Akemi, our host. Kate and I were taken with her sensibility and charm. Kate composed a magnificent letter to say thank you to everybody as we had been looked after with such grace and care.

In 1977 I ran a big workshop in Ararat Regional Gallery with my friend Pamela Gullifer, who has now passed away and is much missed. On that day we must have had hundreds of people, children and adults. It all went smoothly and with lots of smiles all over the place like red poppies in the field, shining.

I did a workshop in the Geelong Art Gallery also. Students love to work near beautiful paintings and sculptures. And I did several workshops in the Wool Museum, where visitors could linger and be a good audience. The visitors came to see a doll fair on show adjacent to our space during the two days of our workshop, an embroidery one. I launched the doll fair and my fees disappeared again in two little dolls that I love.

I did a workshop at Mietta's, in the Queenscliff Hotel, organised by the CAE. I had just returned from my second trip to France and I was very tired. I needed to drink stout for strength. We had great dinners and lunches and very attentive waiters. As Melbourne was calling for me, many students decided to stay a few more days by themselves and continued to work in their hotel room with passion. It had been a great success.

Bendigo Art School invited me to do a workshop. The college art collection had an Arnold Shore painting of a garden which I loved. Arnold Shore had given me my very first review in the *Age* in the fifties. He died soon after. It was a favourable critique and, being from a fellow painter, I was much honoured. I remember his fine silhouette as I saw him walking towards me in the Fitzroy Gardens as he made *ma connaissance*.

In Sydney, at the Pavilion, a stunning workshop was organised. As I worked, a brilliant journalist interviewed me: Sandra Hall. One is only as good as the interviewer. She had asked me, 'What is a doll?' or something like that. In a kind of bravado, my answer was what Freud once wrote: 'A doll is a penis replacement.' I did feel embarrassed when the interview was also printed in the *Age*, but no one blinked an eye. Other times, other morals: *autres temps, autres moeurs*.

Mildura was another heavenly workshop, with all the magnolia trees in flower – long streets of them. The flowers come first and then the leaves. Thinking about Murray Bail's novel, *Eucalyptus*,

I wonder how many species of magnolia trees there are. In Mildura, the *Magnolia grandiflora* were quite spectacular, with scented, creamy flowers. The smaller trees we see in Melbourne have always enchanted me. It was a French botanist, Pierre Magnol, 1638–1715, whose name was given to the trees.

Two sisters of a certain age, dressed in black and large – not unlike the ladies of my childhood in Saint-James who gave me dragées – sat next to each other in Mildura. They came to make a doll each, not really interested in what I was showing. I did not insist, noticing they were having such pleasure making two lovely identical little dolls that I wished I had – Victorian dolls, dressed meticulously with perfectly painted faces.

In Wodonga, another workshop with a student whose husband had a great wine cellar. We drank his wine; it was a very civilised workshop, with art, good food, wine, lively students, summertime, all mature women.

Another workshop I ran in a tiny school, in a tiny country town, whose art teacher took an instant dislike to me. The headmaster was very disconcerted, but made sure I did my work with the students all the same. After three days' work, as I went to my motel in a cab, through the little town, crying, I saw all along the main road children clutching the dolls they had made with me. I was happy though I was still crying, watching them, boys and girls going home with their new treasures.

Here I am crying now as I write these words. I didn't speak to the art teacher at all. Actually, I remember that after a workshop I usually cry. It is an anticlimax when the party is over, as I like my workshops to be a kind of party where you have learning adventures.

I remember a very popular workshop in the Burnie Library,

Tasmania. It went on for several days, and years later people are still talking about it, I was told at a workshop in Devonport in 1997. The Devonport workshop was held in a church, transformed into a gallery. The impact of the church was still there, uncannily, when we walked into the vestibule. Many artists were showing there and my two friends from Devonport, Stephanie and Elizabeth, had organised the workshop. My friend Sheilah Wood had come from Launceston with a friend to participate in the workshop.

In Devonport I stayed in a bed and breakfast where dolls and toys were exhibited in glass cases. In the morning I could see the Mersey River through the trees and a large white boat three decks high sailing extremely slowly through the trees. It was an erotic experience – a metamorphic trap I fall for everytime, and great cause for laughter sometimes.

Another beautiful workshop in Daylesford. There I was in the train at Spencer Street Station looking at the departure time on the platform, and my train not moving. I went out of my compartment to look at the platform clock again, through the door this time, putting my head out, looking to the right and the left, when I saw the front of the train, where I should have been, leaving. I was stranded with the part of the train that stayed on the platform, a late afternoon by then and winter.

I still made it to Daylesford that night, by trains and taxis. Outside my hotel window, lots of koalas having a party right through the night. They didn't let me sleep but I loved their grunts of pleasure. It was a beautiful workshop organised by the city of Daylesford and a brilliant sculptor, Lorraine Jenyns.

Recalling Bairnsdale, the town where Hal Porter was born and where David Williamson was a little boy in one of the classrooms, where a gang of very good painters came to work with me. It was from the window of the Riversleigh Hotel where I stayed often, on the edge of the Mitchell River, that I had a great painting experience. It was a kind of optical illusion – nature's observations are good for that – the shining river was reflecting itself on the tummies of large birds flying over the river, lit by the afternoon sun, still high in the sky. Birds flying over the river and birds disappearing in the trees, losing the shine off their tummies and confusing me no end: one minute a shining bird and next minute it is gone.

At Shepparton I gave workshops in a lovely school, the Goulburn Valley Grammar School, and in the regional gallery who had at the time a grand Longstaff portrait of Mrs George Lansell, of Bendigo fame, for sale. I loved it very much.

Twice I was artist-in-residence at Geelong Grammar School – ten days, large workshops. Once, I had nineteen boys and one girl at a doll-making lesson. I was very intrigued not to have more seventeen-year-old girls. As I spoke to their teacher, we agreed to have a conversation workshop – a tea party – next day to catch the missing students of the previous day. All the girls came. They were very preoccupied about their future and wanted to know about my life as a painter.

In an Eaglehawk high school near Bendigo, Maureen Power, a teacher, organised fabulous workshops with teenagers. We painted a mural in the corridor of the school in playing cards of all sizes and all kinds. Usually, I stayed in a hotel or motel but this time I stayed with Maureen Power and her husband. Their house was full of toys and dolls, and a studio for porcelain doll making was very well equipped. It was delightful to be a guest. The country all around was again calling me, 'Paint me, paint me.'

Beautiful workshops were run at Heide Museum of Modern Art. Schools came, pretty ladies came, and Maudie Palmer, then the director of MOMA, was very grateful for the money raised to support the museum.

A Swan Hill workshop was enchanting, with a charming man wearing a large white moustache and much romance about him. I almost forgot the workshop and my reason for being in Swan Hill. We could have gone away on the beautiful Murray River, on a barge somewhere.

There were many gigantic workshops at the National Gallery of Victoria, where more and more art teachers came and children also; I like mixing all ages. My way of teaching was different for adults and children. Children can do no wrong and everything they do deserves praise. Sometimes, when children come to my classes, I invite them to be little teachers with me and help to show the adults how to go about their work. The smiles on the children's beautiful faces as they become little teachers! The adults become magic also.

I led workshops in people's townhouses and people's summer houses, in little galleries in Melbourne town. I would rarely say no to a workshop and arrived by bicycle or taxi or tram or aeroplane – tiny little planes who left their morning shadows on the landscape. Once I came back from Horsham in a little two-seater plane – I didn't want to go by train. There was the pilot, one student sitting next to the pilot and myself sitting behind the pilot. As we climbed and travelled nicely, the door next to the student opened and could not be shut. The pilot, who had a map on his knees and held the wheel lovingly, calmed my coming worry – we descended to a minute Ararat aerodrome, lonesome in the middle of nowhere. The door was *grosso modo* fixed and we climbed up again, the landscape so close. Soon, I saw the outline of Melbourne and we landed at Essendon airport. I asked the pilot the name of the plane's motor but he didn't know. He had flown six times before and was a very cool, charming pilot, who had learnt in Horsham. Most of that workshop's students were farmers' wives and their strength and good spirit were an inspiration to me.

Canberra, where I held a workshop in the middle of a great *magasin*, catching passers-by. Once, a large group of disabled people came with their teacher who asked if her group could join. I said yes, of course; we organised a way to work and every student painted something on cloth, we doubled it, and with helpers we sewed them on the machine. Some handicapped students joyfully worked on the machine, then each student filled up the painted little bags with soft wool; more helpers were needed to seal the bags and fun was had by all.

Another time, I was invited in Canberra to a very modern school, and yet another time to Art in the Park: each painting was part of a street and it became very real in the park as the children had brilliant ideas in painting, reproducing various shops in the street. This workshop had been a great challenge; with good teachers and lovely students, a lovely park and good weather, you could not miss. A very fine journalist understood my approach to work with children of all ages and wrote an article which I treasure.

I failed to grasp an opportunity for a workshop in Darwin – I regret it to this day, but in the eighties I didn't like to cancel one workshop to do another. Later I learned to cancel workshops when I was in the middle of a large commission and everyone understood.

I loved having workshops in East Melbourne in the studio that was once the home of Ola Cohn, the sculptor who created the fairy tree in the Fitzroy Gardens in Melbourne. Long ago, she had lived at 9 Collins Street. Moving through history is something I love. Places that vibrate still with past events and people and animals and

plants and dust and slugs, like those at 9 Collins Street appearing
without fail after midnight.

An interesting workshop was organised by Paula Fox, the wife
of Lindsay Fox, and Mary Moran at the suggestion of Paula's
daughter Lisa. It was in a cabaret for the American Young President Organisation who had a chapter in Melbourne. It was a great
success, and eerie to work in a cabaret during the daytime. Very
brilliant people came. One charming man understood my ideas and
did the workshop for his twelve-year-old daughter back in the
USA, to show her my technique of doll making. One lady student
who was an Australian and married to an American man bought
some of my work, and when I visited my new friends I could see
my work well loved in a house bathed in natural light and with
many children by the seaside in California.

In one workshop I had in Geelong for a week, a ravishing old
lady asked me every day to come to her place. As a rule I don't go
visiting or out during a workshop, as I would lose the spell of conducting the workshop. The last day I agreed. During the week, she
had said she wanted to show me something special, but would not
say what it was.

The night of the visit arrived and her husband kindly collected
me at my hotel. It was a full moon, we drove through a haunting
landscape like one of the night paintings Charles Blackman did in
the fifties at Avonsleigh. He used to run off into the night when
Gray Smith chased him with a gun after quarrelling.

I could see quite a large stark white building in the distance. It
was a Guilford Bell house, impeccably beautiful. The surprise was
a large trunk full of heirloom lace which had just arrived from
London. In the collection was lace I had studied in my books, particularly *Lace: A History*, by Santina M. Levey. In the trunk were

the pieces I had been dribbling over in ecstasy in this book. My hosts were impressed with my knowledge of early sixteenth-century Italian lace, which I love especially. Lace is closely linked to embroidery and also the great paintings of the time; endless lace was painted on the portraits of kings and queens, infants and great people, men and women. I told my hosts to contact the National Gallery of Victoria as a good curator could help write about such marvels in the trunk. I was well rewarded, after the insistence by the lady all week had puzzled me.

More workshops in Tasmania, organised by John Thorp, who once worked for the Council of Adult Education and whose long letters to entice me to come once more I cherish. It was Cliff Pugh's idea for John to organise those workshops after he retired from the CAE. The workshops were called Adventures in Art, and I did seven or eight of them altogether. Hobart was to be a great doll workshop with lots of interesting people. One student was a doctor; I asked her one day if she knew where there could be antique dolls. She promptly said that she knew where there were two. Eagerly I suggested that we go after class to look at them.

In the antique shop two large beautiful dolls stared at us. One was a porcelain doll, the other was made of wax over composition, very old. I straight away loved the wax one – quite damaged by many Australian hot summers, but haunting. As we talked with the antique dealer of the origins of the wax doll, we found out that she once belonged to the family of my student, on her mother's side. Regretfully, I thought my student should have the first option on the wax doll and I bought the other large baby doll, German-made, with starry blue eyes with lashes, authentic clothes and leather shoes. Lashes on dolls fascinated me as a child.

After the workshop, I went home very sad to leave the other

doll. Back in Melbourne, for one year I dreamt of the wax doll I called Corina, Corinne in French. Corinne was a lovely French girl working with Monsieur Renard in his Paris boutique. I often spoke to her on the telephone as I bought dolls from Monsieur Renard, *spécialiste de poupées, automates et jouets anciens*. George Baldessin brought me a poster from Monsieur Renard's, I had asked him to get one for me. My son William went to the boutique to look at a doll I wanted and purchased it. William photographed the lovely shop and its display of dolls for me.

By the time I got back to Paris, Monsieur Renard had died. I still went straight to 6 rue de l'Echaudé where the boutique was. No more dolls. Another owner. I also went the same day to Sennelier's, quai Malaquais, where Cézanne bought his paints. I was ecstatic and had an instant nervous colic. I went to the very, very old WC of Sennelier's and I nearly died with pain, but I loved the very old WC with its pulling chain, like my old one at Barkly Street, St Kilda. *Ça me tue*, just looking at the correspondence and photos of dolls I craved for and got, and a photo of old Sennelier's paint shop.

One year later, I was again invited to conduct a workshop in Hobart and I was hoping against hope the doll might still be there. In the early morning upon my return, I went to the antique shop to gaze in. The doll was still there and the same student was again in my workshop class. At lunch I went and bought the doll, thinking it was ethical having waited one year. The doctor student had bought a dresser instead and thought it was more useful, even though she had four daughters.

I made research on the doll with the help of John Thorp, who took me to the homestead where the doll once lived. The doll had come to Hobart in 1837 with the Butler family who had come from England. In the book *Wainewright in Tasmania*, by Robert Crossland,

TOP Sunday Reed at Heide, 1960

BOTTOM Albert Tucker and me in the house
of photographer Brian McArdle, circa 1961

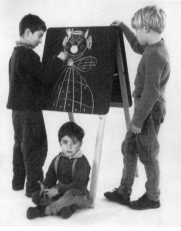

TOP Holding Tiriel at 9 Collins Street, with William and Philippe next to me

ABOVE LEFT With Philippe and William (who is one month old) outside 9 Collins Street, 1950

ABOVE RIGHT (L to R) Philippe drawing a clown, William thinking, Simon Wynn watching, Melbourne, 1956

OPPOSITE With a pen-and-ink drawing at the Balzac, 1960

LEFT Tiriel and Alice Perceval in their drawer-boats, Aspendale, 1960

BELOW (L to R) Winkie Perceval, me, Tiriel, Alice Perceval, Mary Perceval, Aspendale, 1961

OPPOSITE TOP With Tiriel and his flute, Melbourne, 1962

OPPOSITE BOTTOM William in front of my painting *Mother and Child*, 1962

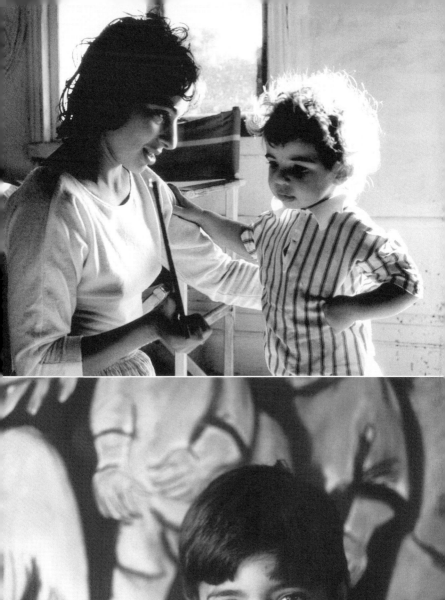

OPPOSITE TOP Tiriel playing at being Marlon Brando, 1963

OPPOSITE BOTTOM Philippe underneath one of his drawings, 1963

ABOVE The family in my studio at Tolarno. (L to R) Philippe, me, William, Tiriel (on the ladder), Georges. Tiriel was shy as a little boy so I got him his own ladder to sit on. That way he was taller than the adults and could see what was happening. It worked beautifully

ABOVE Meeting Marcel Marceau again after many years, Melbourne, 1963. Marcel, then on his first Australian tour, was being interviewed for ABC television. I hid behind a curtain in the studio, and at a prearranged signal appeared as a surprise. I hadn't seen Marcel since leaving Paris

LEFT Marcel Marceau designed this soft sculpture of his famous character, Bip. I cut it out, sewed and filled it, and Marcel painted it

ABOVE This photo of me appeared in an exhibition at Georges Department Store in 1969. It was taken by Dr Geoffrey Smith, a dentist by profession, who photographed Melbourne's most beautiful women for his show

LEFT On the cover of *Oz* magazine, 1964

OPPOSITE TOP (L to R) Philippe, my father, William, in my father's Paris apartment, 1972

OPPOSITE LEFT Philippe with Dennis Hopper on the set of *Mad Dog Morgan*, 1976

OPPOSITE RIGHT Philippe directing Tiriel, who played a punk in *Captain Invincible*, Sydney, 1982

ABOVE Me with duck, Melbourne, 1972

ABOVE With my soft sculptures, 1978

LEFT With a friend in my house at Wellington Street, 1971

OPPOSITE TOP My three French dolls, bought in Paris from Monsieur Renard's shop

OPPOSITE BOTTOM At work at Barkly Street, 1988

OPPOSITE TOP At the Four Winds concert in Bermagui, 1997. (L to R) Carrillo and Neilma Gantner, Margaret and Gough Whitlam, and an unknown boy who befriended me

OPPOSITE LEFT William making a speech at my exhibition at his Flinders Lane gallery, 1997

OPPOSITE RIGHT With Tiriel at dinner, Melbourne, 1997

ABOVE (L to R) Tiriel, Philippe, me, William at my retrospective, Museum of Modern Art, Heide, 1999

LEFT With Betty Churcher at my retrospective, Museum of Modern Art, Heide, 1999

Publicity shot for my exhibition at Mary Place
Gallery in Sydney, 1996

I found the portraits of the three sisters who once played with the doll and looked after the doll. Thomas Griffiths Wainewright had been a convict painter and writer but his life in Tasmania was without stain and he was trusted to paint the portraits of many families.

The doll has cobalt eyes, arms and legs half in wax and half in cloth, and still wears her original underpants. The eyes move when a little wire at the back of the doll's waist is activated. Sometimes little animals nibble at her in my house in Barkly Street as she sits on my bed instead of being locked up in a cupboard, or on top of a wardrobe as she did for so many years in Hobart. I wrote a letter once to the very great expert on dolls, E.A. Coleman, who wrote back kindly. She was quite familiar with my doll and placed her as being born in England, circa 1820.

The fees of my workshops never covered my dolls' expenses and John Thorp was quite perturbed by my behaviour, to say the least. I felt very strange with the wax doll flying over Bass Strait, where she would have travelled on a sailing ship in 1837. These kinds of sensations are rare and dislocate you.

There is another workshop I remember with great emotion. It was a workshop for dancers at the School of Dance in the Victorian College of the Arts, Melbourne. Their delicacy in approaching their work was a great lesson to me. We made masks, putting tissue paper over a clay mould the dancers had moulded and then painting the tissue paper daintily.

A workshop at my son's gallery gave me the best fees ever. It was a family affair and my friend Carol Schwartz and her husband organised a birthday party workshop. It was a great success and lovely to have a father and mother along with the children to make dolls or just play with colours. Fathers usually shied away from workshops. At that workshop I realised I could not see the hole in the machine's needle. Suddenly, I was confronted with time running out.

I am almost forgetting the summer school workshops at the CAE. They were so interesting as they lasted several days; this would allow more time to go into depth with the various subjects we were tackling, and great results were achieved and champagne drunk at the end party.

One workshop the CAE organised had artists and craftspeople in a train stopping at different stations for the day. At Castlemaine station, I painted with three hundred people on several boards attached to the train. I had outlined some of my motifs for them to work with. People added something to the work right through the day. At night, when everybody had left and I was lucky enough to have a bright moonlight, I reorganised the mural as best I could. It now hangs on the second floor of the CAE building in Flinders Street, Melbourne. It is a happy sight, even though people didn't approve of me letting other people embellish my own work. Sometimes an entire family would work on the mural.

Most workshops gave me a lot of pleasure at seeing people discovering their artistic potential. One workshop that got me so moved, and at times flummoxed, was a doll workshop at the old Pentridge Jail; I could not distinguish the jailed from the jailers at first. When the students started to work with me, it was easier. Every person drew a bird, some little birds, some larger, and some much larger, like eagles. We cut them out from drawing paper, put the patterns on cloth, sewed them with a sewing machine or by hand, stuffed them with acrylic wool, and there you had a little or large soft sculpture, ready to be painted.

The men painted their birds and were so happy to have achieved something. In their minds, the birds could fly in and out of the windows. I am thinking of Ovid the poet who wrote in his *Metamorphoses* that though everything else in the universe is subject to change and dissolution, the soul alone is exempt from this law – in *Metamorphoses*, this is Pythagoras's great speech.

I loved reading Ovid and Virgil when I was a young girl of sixteen. Poor Ovid was sent in exile for his daring poetry, which displeased Augustus. Ovid died in exile at Tomis, Romania, the country of my maternal grandparents. Ovid was born in Sulmo in 43BC and died seventeen years after the birth of Christ. His name in Latin was Publius Ovidius Naso. Ovid, the last of the love elegists.

Another workshop in Queensland was part of a large festival in Maroochydore. I had to start the day early and often I was too tired to. In the early morning I would hear a didgeridoo played by an Aboriginal man, and I would at once jump out of my bed and walk to the sound, refreshed and full of life again: an ancient call buried in my brain that I could recognise, atavistic. Many people came from Brisbane as my workshops, with time, became very popular.

One workshop in Campbell Town, near Launceston, was at a place called The Grange. The homestead once belonged to my old friend Rosemary Ryan's family. There had been a dramatic love story attached to it. John Thorp again organised this workshop, which meant it would be civilised, with morning coffee, afternoon tea and many dinner parties. It was to be a painting workshop. I asked for two models, one a very old lady and the other an old man. The old lady knew many stories and the old man was the local priest, who loved being painted.

One intriguing young romantic man was painting a bride and was thinking about an interesting young woman. I thought that at the final dinner I would sit next to him as he was wearing very classic shoes, very elegant; I thought that if he was wearing these fine shoes he would order good wine. He did. Ray and I became great friends and he did marry Louise, the young woman he was thinking about, and a most captivating daughter was born to them, Sophie.

In Launceston, I found my friends Sheilah Wood and her husband. A great dinner party for overseas visitors and myself ensued. Sheilah Wood had not lost her touch as each visitor looked most enigmatic, like in a John le Carré novel.

As I climbed that night on board a late flight for Melbourne, a man sat next to me completely engrossed in reading a John le Carré book. I felt quite uneasy, as a writer would not think of that little end scenario in the plane. Had it been the afternoon or morning I would have reacted differently, but the night is a sorceress.

MY COMMISSIONS

uite often, when I am at home working at my *chevalet* – my easel – I dream to have a large commission. When I have a large commission, I dream to be at home at my *chevalet*. But maybe I like most being at my *chevalet* working at new discoveries about handling the paint, and finding new evocative images that tantalise me, puzzle me. Somehow each commission is the sum total of all my discoveries. That is why I love to be at my *chevalet*, mostly to stock up on my ideas.

The Flinders Street Station project was offered to seven painters to submit their ideas for decorating the wall at the end of the concourse in Swanston Street. Six brilliant painters, male, and one brilliant female painter (*moi*). I thought I didn't have a chance, but all the same went to look at the wall, and as I looked at the wall I said to myself, 'This wall is mine,' feeling like an animal. Had I been a dog, I would have peed on it.

Without telling anyone, I disappeared for three days and three nights at the Windsor Hotel and in great comfort I designed the mural just as you see it now. I was pleased and drank champagne, my mind running fast. When I came home, I looked at my three volumes of *French Sculptors of the 17th and 18th Centuries: The Reign of Louis XIV*, an illustrated catalogue by François Souchal. I can and have spent many hours looking at it, and there I found a mural just the same as my design I gave birth to at the Windsor Hotel: a painted frieze at the top, one by nine metres; a mosaic two by nine metres in the centre; and a low relief at the bottom, one by nine metres. I was pleased like a cat who just drank fresh cream.

The project was organised by the Ministry of the Arts and the Ministry of Transport. At the station, on the first floor above the lovely clocks, was the office of the station manager, and next to it a large room for architects and myself and many other people who looked after me as if I was a precious stone, especially Mr Kudlicki who protected me from a suggestion of a door being made right through the middle of the mural. It didn't happen.

It was the time of many strikes, 1985–86, and both the unions and the government were kind to me and my assistant Nicola. The River Garden was the restaurant adjacent to the mural and I went there often to eat lobsters, and I still feel guilty as I saw them alive and would choose one to eat. Once, after choosing another live lobster to eat, I had a dream about the sea's soul and I understood a little more about the sea, its life as a being of some kind. It was an important dream: the sea as a body and a universe. It left me like Saint-Exupéry's little prince on his little star, far away from the earth.

So good to work inside a big scaffold, right in the city, and feel the heartbeat of Melbourne: protest marches, celebrations, strikes, the weather, summer, winter, autumn, springtime, people passing by – mostly very curious, and good praise came often. John Cain, the Premier, came to look at my progressing work. Patrick McCaughey, the director of the National Gallery of Victoria, danced for me as he passed by. Now many lovers from all around the world come to Melbourne and have their photo taken in front of the station mural. Little children love to put their fingers in the carved lines of the low relief, as I knew they would. In 1986 I signed my name with mosaic at the completion of the mural.

The very first commission I remember was creating the set and costumes for *Ivan the Terrible*, a Rex Reid ballet, in 1964. The lighting in the theatre was very poor and the gold I used right through the throne and icons and costumes saved the show a little as it reflected the light. Asher Bilu had introduced me to Plaka Casein paints; I used them a lot on theatre sets and costumes and dolls and embroideries.

My friend Pamela Gullifer came one day to my studio and enticed me to create an exhibition of embroideries, seventeen in all, to travel through many regional galleries. The fees were good; of course every gallery wanted to buy the embroideries, but I kept them all as they were unique and one could never make them again. Instead, I conducted many embroidery workshops and many students of all ages did wonderful work using my method.

Painting my first tram, in 1978, was a great folly as I had sore arms for eight months afterwards, and so did other painters bigger than me. It was lovely to see the tram going through the streets of Melbourne and the paintings reflected in the shop windows. As it passed through the various suburbs it looked different in style, depending on the architectural background of diverse *époques*, old and new.

For some reason, I wanted my tram to look white from a distance, and as it approached I wanted the colours to unveil themselves. I used very few: red, green, black and white. Just four colours. After rereading Brent Berlin and Paul Kay's book, *Basic Color Terms, Their Universality and Evolution*, I found that right throughout the world red is the most known colour, also green, black for night and white for day. I wanted to read about primitive people's notion of colours, and in many parts of the world people have smaller or larger vocabularies for colours. The book by Berlin and Kay helped me a lot in tackling the painting of the tram without losing the content of my images. I was interested in the limited vocabulary of colours as the tram was for the people in the street. But of course, with a few colours you can produce millions of nuances, describing air, mood, passion. My white stood for yellows, my black for blues, red for browns, hiding in browns. Green was itself. It was extremely interesting.

The day came when the tram was to go out into the world and from far away it looked white and as it came closer the colours unveiled themselves. I was so pleased – it was almost a miracle, my palette was very restrained but it worked.

I remember a summer day standing at the corner of Little Collins Street and Swanston Street as my tram passed; an elderly gentleman stopped by me to praise the painted tram and tell me how much pleasure it gave him.

During 1979–80, I was asked to design sets, costumes and masks for the plays *Medea* and *Bacchae* by Euripides, directed by Murray Copland for the Playbox Theatre. It was to be an enormous work, and great fun to work with the actors and costume makers. The producer, Sandy Mattlock, was extraordinarily patient with me as I don't comprehend space and could only design sets *in situ*, and ended up having many entrances and exits for the actors. I could not draw on my flat page – uncanny. Both plays were a great success and the drawings and costumes and masks are now held at the National Gallery of Australia, Canberra, and the Performing Arts Museum, Melbourne.

In March 1999 I had the chance to see some of the *Medea* masks again when they were on loan to the Bendigo Art Gallery. I hardly dared look at them as they would awaken so many tumultuous memories. I was very honoured to have been asked to open the exhibition in Bendigo, which was called *Dress Rehearsals and the Wig Room*. I was to make a very short speech, which is the hardest to do as you have to find images that people will remember for a long time. I took one image from after a performance of *Medea*, when we would answer questions to school students – Murray Copland and myself sitting on the proscenium facing the students. One little girl, who noticed the messenger had no clothes under his flying cloak as he ran, asked, 'Why are the actors naked under their clothes?' I answered, 'We are all naked under our clothes.' Now when I go to the theatre I remember the little girl's question and see all the spectators naked under their clothes.

The other image came from those nights when everyone had left my studio and I was in the dark with all the masks reflecting the lane's lights, a blue light, and I would go into a slumber and go to sleep with Euripides. A lady approached me after my speech and said she was the niece of Ola Cohn, the sculptor who once lived in 9 Collins Street. As a child, visiting her aunt's studio and sleeping there, she remembered the sculptures being lit by the street's lamps and being haunted. In those days the lights were yellow.

I spoke to many people who loved the costumes and wigs and masks and who I knew from long ago, remembering their faces but not always their names. A big dinner was organised at the Shamrock Hotel by the Director of the Bendigo Art Gallery, Mr Tony Ellwood, in my honour and that of the two curators.

And now it is 1.20pm, 7th March 1999, and I am sitting in the train who leaves soon for Melbourne. I dream and write and I think of Marlborough House where I stayed that night, in Wattle Road, Bendigo and its history of last century. Footsteps in the night of ghosts I thought I heard. I noticed the house looked like a little 'Fortuna', the house of George Lansell, Bendigo's 'Quartz King'. As I spoke to the new owner of Marlborough House I learnt that it had been built in 1889 and had been designed by Vahland, the architect who did the extensions for 'Fortuna'. Art and architecture always potent, sending messages.

Later, I was to work again with Murray Copland for the Bicentennial festivities. It was on an opera, *Bennelong*, about the intriguing Aboriginal man who was befriended by Captain Phillip. Bennelong was taken to London and back again and met a tragic death. My son William found an engraving of Bennelong and it lives in my bedroom. The painter Churchill Cann, who had an exhibition at William's gallery in May 1998, reminded me of Bennelong in character. Churchill was and is a very profound man, a performer so jolly and a true artist, singing and dancing to amuse his admirers.

The opera, with libretto by Murray Copland and musical score by Barry Conyngham, was shown at the Sydney Opera House where the Sydney Chamber Orchestra performed the music, in Melbourne at the Concert Hall, later in Brisbane and then in Holland. I didn't go to Holland as I was too tired and I regret it, missing out on seeing their museums' collections of masters. I designed many five-foot-high puppets on plywood, all painted with oil, eighty-five in all. Lucy Osborne, who was to become my daughter-in-law by marrying my son William, was my assistant. In Sydney she had worked with Martin Sharp and studied art. She has an impeccable eye. She was then very young and beautiful, and still is. Her talent for drawing from life is more than excellent, say I with envy.

We designed the personages first, and with an electric saw cut them out. They had to be covered evenly with good gesso and then painted. My palette was large as a table and someone took it home at the end, after asking me for it. I wish I had the palette now as it was a giant one.

As I was designing a sailing boat, everyone laughed about me but Barry Conyngham wanted the boat. The laughing was because I made the boat go one way and the sails the other. Once I found out about the cause of so much laughter, I made a second boat going the right way, with its blown sails following the prow this time.

I have a splendid Dutch poster with the Bennelong participants and my name as the puppet designer. John Beckett constructed the large kind of Punch and Judy theatre box, very large as the puppets were so gigantic and three puppeteers were needed. It was the size of the orchestra who determined the size of the puppets – the birth of ideas intrigues me. We received great praise for the Bennelong opera in Australia, and won the Sounds Australia Award in 1993: the Critics' Award for the Best Musical was presented to Barry Conyngham for his puppet opera *Bennelong*, with libretto by Murray Copland and puppets by Mirka Mora.

One little commission that I enjoyed, as I could do it *in situ*, was a mural for the first floor at the CAE. Two or three students could help me as well as part of their work experience. This mural had to be in the context of the CAE. In moments like that, I go to my beloved book by Cesare Ripa: *Baroque and Rococo Pictorial Imagery 1758–60*. *Iconologia* with two hundred engraved illustrations. I think of a word, say, 'intelligence', and there it is in the book as a lady with wings on her head, and off I go and do it my way. It is a bit like tarot cards: think of a word and see images in your mind and the cards (one of my tricks) and choose. I am thinking of the very rare nineteenth-century Mademoiselle Lenormand cards which my husband Georges bought at a flea market in Paris for me.

A lovely commission my dear late friend Carole Parker gave me was to paint a mural on an entire wall of her sitting room. The wall was pale green and I kept the colour as a background. Carole Parker worked for *Vogue* and fought for art, was adamant to have my erotic charcoal series printed in the *Vogue* magazine in the early seventies, an entire page of drawings. Carole died later, very suddenly, of cancer and I was so sad to see fear in her eyes. Her very nice nanny came to one of my exhibition openings and we could reminisce and be photographed together, trying to catch time past.

The pavilion at the end of the St Kilda pier was to have a mosaic, a kind of map of St Kilda. It was part of the view from my house in Barkly Street through to the sea, past Luna Park, the Palais, the Esplanade Hotel, and so on. Walking inside my work. It was a few months after an operation I was recovering from and I thought it better to be there, in the windy pavilion, than in my bed. I pretended to myself I was sailing on many a cold and windy day. A cubby-house was built for my tools and materials, but I never trusted it and it was eventually broken into. I had a charming assistant, Olivia, with a car; I thought it an imposition every day putting my tools and luggage in her car as she would kindly offer to pick me up. I preferred to be free. I thought of taxis but the fees would have been enormous. I also had leg pains that came and that no one could help me with. I had been to various doctors but to no avail. So I decided to buy the best pram in town (as I love prams) and put my mosaic materials and tools and books and camera in it and walk from home to the pavilion in the morning and from the pavilion to my home at night.

I could reassess my work along the road – that is, look at Luna Park again and the Esplanade Hotel with its long history of famous guests: Sarah Bernhardt, Mr Felton of the Felton Bequest, with his friend Mr Grimwade visiting him. It sure cured my mysterious leg pains and on the way home, often walking along the sea, I would get good painting lessons in greys and would stop at Jean-Jacques restaurant to have a good meal and go straight to bed when home, after preparing the next day's work.

I wanted the mosaic to capture the shining waves in daytime, which meant I liked the mosaic pieces in the plaster put on an angle to catch the light. It was hard to do. Sometimes, with the right sunshine, the mosaic would scintillate like the sea. Rainy days would clean the mosaic and make it shiny. We saw, my assistant and I, all the residents with dogs taking their pets for a walk; we saw fathers taking their young sons sailing, sometimes a daughter. We saw many lovely people watching us work, many tourists from all around the world. A French group of people came and I pretended that I didn't speak French as I wanted to hear what they said about my work. They admired it. Once I was in Sydney, at a bar, drawing. There were two French men speaking to each other; again I didn't say I spoke French and could overhear their remarks. They thought my work was lascivious and I was pleased but kept silent.

Another time, a German group of tourists passed the pavilion and looked. I could hear their tour leader say, 'It is real art, Kunst.' I was very moved and kept working. People came from South America, from Spain, from LA, from Japan. It gave me a different aspect of St Kilda, being visited by so many people from overseas.

One day a beautiful Chinese bride and groom were photographed at the pavilion. It was a windy day and the white veil of the bride floating was like a caress on the pavilion, or a very pretty butterfly on its way to love. Butterflies can travel eleven kilometres to find their love mate.

Many seagulls came, but I never saw a cat. Little pigeons came. Once, Caroline Ross and Claudia Wright, both outstanding journalists, came with Claudia's mother. It was an outing for Claudia and I managed to make her laugh, even though her illness, Alzheimer's disease, was well advanced.

Another time, a doctor, a most charming man of a certain age, came in a Rolls-Royce with a most delicious mother, elderly and chic. As I'd recently had an operation this doctor asked me who had operated on me. I told him the name of my surgeon, Professor Michael Quinn, and the charming man said, 'I taught the boy.' I felt quite safe. He also gave me his name and address, he wrote in one of my drawing books while his mother was looking at me very carefully, like possessive mothers do.

Many years ago Clyde Packer gave me a lovely commission for an apartment he had in East Melbourne. There was a wall I could paint to my heart's delight and a lovely butler to attend to my every need. Clyde went away overseas. The butler, most of the time, would sunbake on his tummy and I thought he had a lovely bottom, but someone had to paint the mural and it was me. The mural was quite large and high, covered with lovers, birds, foliage – colourful and tender. I was quite elated with it as it is always a kind of surprise to have accomplished a work, and agreeable to be pleased. When Clyde Packer came back he had to see a psychiatrist to see why the mural made him so happy.

He later bought a large painting he loved and said it was so spaced out. It was the one I entered in the 1968 Invitation Prize, held at Georges department store in Collins Street. I didn't win. Clyde took it with him to Los Angeles where he lives and invited my son Philippe for lunch to show him a surprise. He opened two doors and there was my painting – the surprise.

To Perth in 1983, where I was commissioned to paint a long mural on metal prepared for paint; it was outside the Concert Hall and during the Perth Festival. I had a very good assistant there also, Judith. I studied as much as I could about the history of Perth and I came across a story of a shipwreck full of ladies who all survived, also a good nun story, and many more stories. Dame Mary Durack came often to make sure that I would not forget to include the Aboriginal people so I painted wandjinas. Martin Sharp had told me about them and, years before that, the writer Alan Marshall at 9 Collins Street had also told me about them and suggested that my work had some Aboriginal dreaming. Once, Clifford Possum saw my work at Andrzej and Grazyna's (who own Coloursquare Framing) and said, 'I can read Mirka's dreaming.' I was so pleased. Art is universal.

Clifton Pugh and his partner Adriana were in town and Adriana photographed my mural. Cliff was then painting the portrait of Robert Holmes à Court. His beautiful wife came in to shake hands. One day a car stopped outside the mural as I was working and Charles Blackman came out with a new wife and two children. Charles at the time was designing a ballet set in Perth.

People in Perth were very kind. They brought me food or took me for lunch, and one day I left my boots at the restaurant, to the amazement of the other guests, and went back to work shoeless. Just a performance. That very day, a person who was an antique dealer brought me presents: a Punch and Judy porcelain, just the Punch, and a hundred-year-old pair of *bottines* which fitted perfectly. The *bottines* were made of leather from which a distinctive noise emerged. One man fell in love with me because of the squeaky noise the *bottines* made as I walked. I remembered shoe fetishists and was careful: Restif de la Bretonne comes to mind, *écrivain français* 1734–1806.

One day a big black dog came to me with a beautiful bottle of red wine attached to his back with a large ribbon which said 'Mirka'. I never found out who sent it. My hotel was across the road from the mural and one morning as I was painting I realised I was not wearing a skirt, just a pair of Victorian long underpants open in the middle. I quickly went back to my hotel, quite surprised to have been so absent-minded. It means your mind is on your work only – or did I want fresh air on my bottom to clarify my mind?

And then, another day, the wind blew terribly; a kind of hurricane had descended on us, pushing all the pots of paints. I watched them gliding. One of the large pots of paint fell over, emptied itself over the embankment, covering a large part of it. Quickly I designed with my brush a mermaid and this caused a terrible hubbub. The city council cleaners and the cleaners of the

Concert Hall didn't know who was to clean the paint and to whom the mermaid belonged, etc. Just a little havoc in the newspapers for a few days, say I with glee.

Right after I'd finished the mural in Perth I went to Ayr, in Queensland, where I had a commission to decorate the Burdekin Theatre courtyard, who had a long wall, with the help of school-children and passers-by. I also had a commission to do the great mural for the library of Ayr. The mural for the library was my own work but a man helped me with the undercoat. He moved his brush very thoroughly and I became quite aroused watching the regular movement of the brush turning over and over, left and right, up and down.

The man was high up on the open scaffold, nine metres above the ground. I was not aroused any more as I climbed there, a most terrible vertigo invaded me and I started to fart without stopping, until the man left me up there all by myself. To cure my vertigo, I tried to think I was a trapezist. I could not cure my farting when the Lord Mayor came to see me. I was in an abominable situation, what with the noise and smell.

Again, it was fabulous to read about the history of Ayr, about James Murray the sailor and his boat *Peruvian*. James Murray had been saved by Aboriginals and lived to a long age with the first Australians. In the middle of the town was a statue of the painter Russell Drysdale's ancestor.

I was wined and dined by a charming family whose father loved opals and precious stones and had created a kind of labora-tory for them. It was a studio with strange machines to shine stones for an eccentric professor. A lady quite elderly invited me to her garden to see her giant toad, a live one, and later brought me her toad in a jar so I could paint it. I put its portrait in the mural – a big toad. In her garden were very tall avocado trees in fruit. Her garden was a miniature wild rainforest. I loved all the growth – noisy, alive, moist – its scent, and the small door of her back room of her dark house, probably full of bats hanging from her velvet curtains, which I could vaguely see.

The director of the Burdekin Theatre in Ayr was John Young, who gave me both works: the theatre and the mural at the library. John Young had worked in Hobart at the Theatre Royal until it burnt down. He was and is a most interesting man with many ideas and I loved working with him. His mother had been the first male impersonator in Australia, circa 1900. He also had posters of a play starring an actress who was the love of the explorer Robert O'Hara Burke. Burke went to see her perform in this play in Essendon just before leaving for his catastrophic endeavour. Frank Clune years ago had given me the book he had written about Burke and Wills, *Dig*, and earlier Charles Blackman had given me *Dig* also.

In Ayr I worked to exhaustion and on the last day, on my way to the hotel, I developed a terrible diarrhoea that went right through everything – down my legs, skirts, an inferno. I went into a shop to buy some cloth to make myself another dress in the hotel, to go back to Melbourne in by plane.

After Ayr, to Adelaide. Silver Harris, the director of the gallery at Festival Theatre, knew John Young and she gave me a peculiar commission: the making of an extremely long work on transparent plastic – you could paint on either side, a bit like glass painting. It was to celebrate the circus and a play, *Barnum*, which starred Reg Livermore. Thousands of people came to watch me paint. As usual I researched for my work, this time the history of the circus. One of my favourites amongst many favourites was Blondin, the French man who was a great circus star and a rope-walker. One afternoon a group of English people from Scarborough, who were descendants of Blondin, were so pleased to see a painted story about him, there in Adelaide. I took a photograph of the three English people, so happy and surprised to have found their ancestor so far away from their home, celebrated in a painting on plastic.

I also did cut-outs on plywood that were trapezists hanging from the ceiling. Children drew their faces or a face, cut it out, and soon one wall was covered with faces: the circus audience. It must have been Silver Harris's idea. I painted Mazetta's last ride, which was a man hanging from a horse's back; Madame Zazel, who was fired from a monstrous cannon; and clowns and tigers and bears. The Premier, Don Dunstan, came to pay his respects and I was much honoured. Peter Ward, who had written a poem for me in the fifties, was living in Adelaide and I went to see him in his home.

In Paris, one went to the *cirque d'hiver* once a month as a child, and later as an adult I went regularly with my husband. A new show every month was offered. Once we saw Edith Piaf sing at the *cirque d'hiver*. Unforgettable, as she was so small and the *cirque* so large, her voice filling the place totally. I really had a great time painting *la belle Eve* the bearded lady, and the mermaid with a double tail – I think I invented that one. It is related to a peculiar true story of a girl who had two vaginas and two uteri. The doctor told her she was expecting a baby from the left vagina. The girl said, 'You are wrong, Doctor, I made love in the right vagina.' I do have strange books to study. I painted the Revehos; they juggled upside down. I wrote titles on the pictures.

In Adelaide a lady came every day to see me with her three identical giant dogs, pointy-nosed laughing dogs, and they also stared at me like the lady did. I photographed them. Tony Frewing, who was the director of the gallery before Silver Harris, had the idea of asking me to do the circus mural and then he hanged himself. But I love ghosts. The mural was given to a home for disabled people and hangs very high on large windows – a see-through mural.

In 1978 the New South Wales Crafts Board gave me a lovely commission to fill two clear boxes, specially made for me, with painted dolls. One was called *The Bunyip's Paradise* and the other *The Enchanted Garden*. They were toured all around Australia, but not to Melbourne. A couple of years later I saw the two boxes in Sydney, in the foyer of a hotel where the Education Department was holding a three-day seminar. I had been invited and they filmed me working with children and adults. Seeing the two boxes again had been a surprise for me, years later, the dolls so pristine in their transparent boxes of clear plastic. After three days, everyone voted schools obsolete. Many teachers, many speeches, not enough art. One teacher pleaded for money to buy a safer boat as she had to cross every day a river full of crocodiles in a little dinghy to reach her school in Queensland.

My best commission was when Bob Sessions, Publishing Director at Penguin Books, came to ask me to write my autobiography. As I record that memory I am following the movement of my pen, Lorenzo Lotto, capturing my thoughts. I have five more pens – one is called La Pompadour, one is called Honoré de Balzac, one is called Flaubert, one is called Matisse, and the last one is called Slut, because the shape of the pen demands my holding it almost parallel to the paper, whereas the other pens are held more perpendicular to the page. Some have a finer nib, some larger, some smoother, some I run after.

I started to copy out by hand some of my diaries – I have kept a trunk full of them – when my son William noticed piles of writings and me about to drown in them like a bee in honey. William and Bob Sessions came to save me from almost dying and put me on a safer road by pointing out that I was dealing with my archives the wrong way. It was an insane idea to copy my archives but it was still important for me as I tackled my autobiography as if it was a canvas, researching endlessly in my writings and reliving so much. Now I dwell with my memories and check them with my diaries and photographs and drawings and paintings and letters, with strong coffee and good calvados. It is still like climbing Mt Everest but at my own pace: in a high state of capturing the past, making my brain explode, and total despair at facing my mortality but with a sense of great privilege at reliving my life. I am quite bewildered and need to eat a lot of chocolate, the finest. I am off champagne and good wine right now as I feel I am walking along a precipice and I feel so weak physically. I shower myself with Chanel No. 5, as perfume makes me breathe in case I forget to breathe. Some days I don't want to brush my hair, even though I have cut a lot of it off and the remaining is easier to brush. My bones hurt on my back where wings should grow and I could fly to the sun. Icarus attention, the sea. It is good to record one's life even in the midst of bewildering events, like writing love letters and keeping copies of them.

I once made a film with the director David Grieg called *Mirka's Paradise*, filmed on Mt Kosciuszko. It was beautiful to see so much snow; I had forgotten the sounds of mountains, the silence of the snow. Childhood memories were coming back: snow in winter in Paris, cars leaving designs on the snow with their wheels that I could see from my third-floor window. Ice flowers on windows in the mornings, fractals. The little village where we were hiding during the war covered with snow, my father and I going to a meeting chez Madame Fournier. The moon was glaring that night, the same moon which shone over the concentration camp. The village was so still it could crack my heart.

Another film called *Mirka*, by Paul Cox and his students at Prahran College, was a lovely adventure, particularly when a merry-go-round arrived in a park alongside Fitzroy Street in St Kilda and I asked one of the men if I could hold one wooden horse for the film. Gallantly, he unscrewed the horse and gave it to me, and in the film I go away with the horse. The man is smiling in his eyes. I can't forget the expression in the man's eyes. He knew I loved merry-go-rounds and I knew he was a professional man of travelling fairs. I returned the wooden horse to that beautiful man.

Tympanum, at Realities Gallery, was commissioned by Marianne Baillieu and organised by Eve Johnson. Lots has been written about it, by Ronald Millar, Professor Jenny Zimmer in particular, and Ross Lansell; also in *Arts Melbourne*, Vol. 2, No.1, 1977, and on ABC TV. I had a lovely book on French tympanums given to me and my husband by a French consul and the idea came from the book. Roger Kemp, Les Kossatz, George Baldessin, Andrew Sibley and I were to create it. Euphoria. Now the mural lives in the National Gallery of Queensland, Brisbane. It was once in the Melbourne Town Hall but was rejected by a bad lord mayor, then it lived in a store room and then happily went to Queensland. We all received some welcome money, except the two dead painters, Roger Kemp and George Baldessin. Alas.

Three more lovely commissions. The Ardmona mural for the Turnbull family in Shepparton, the Mirka Room at the home of the

Morgan family in Toorak, and the mural for Dr and Mrs Smyth which was eventually hung in the waiting room at his Vermont clinic, in the Melbourne suburbs.

I always forget how hard and long it is to produce a mural, either direct onto the wall or on a canvas hanging as a mural. You have to prepare the subject of the work carefully and always in context of where it will go. The Ardmona mural was to be for a little girl called Rebecca. The Morgans' was to be for the children's play room in their Toorak home. The Vermont mural for the clinic was to be quite large. For the Vermont work, I thought of painting a kind of bestiary of early images; medicine in ancient times used wondrous beasties, lots of foliage. I painted in oil and used lovely colours to capture these images, familiar images, archetypal images.

In the first week of the painting hanging in the waiting room, a woman having a miscarriage blamed it on the painting. I must have indeed tapped into medieval thoughts in my innocent images. I still think it is one of my best achievements. I planned its composition like an alchemist.

The Morgan room was lovely to paint. On the wall your work somehow has more freedom; it is like dancing in a large ballroom, whereas on canvas it is like dancing in a cabaret, close to your partner. We made part of the film *Mirka* at the children's party in that room. I used Plaka Casein paints: easy to apply, lively colours and they dry fast. Four walls was a large effort. I think it was Margaret Stewart who commissioned the Morgan mural for her grandchildren; she became a great collector of my work.

Thinking of a large ballroom, I remember Charles Blackman and myself wandering in the streets in Melbourne at night when we heard music in the Town Hall. We went in to dance, joining the dancers. We had one dance and then we were told to move out.

Somehow we didn't fit, we had too much *joie de vivre*.

The Turnbull mural in Ardmona was painted in a house whose nursery room I occupied. The house was in an orchard. It was great at last to be in the country and paint, bringing the outside inside my painting. One day, I was to paint a pear tree. I went outside to look at a tree and all I could see was an enormous blue sky above. Not a cloud to be seen in the blue, which turned red if I stared at it for too long. I came back into the room to paint the pear tree but I could only capture one blue pear on the tree. I was amazed as the tree was covered with pears. I captured lots of little daily events otherwise, the work in the orchard, the frogs, the dogs, lovers in the trees and also on the motorbike, the little baby Rebecca. And Punch and Judy. It was a lovely work to do and much coffee was drunk from a silver pot. There was also a doll in the painting, to my great delight. Dolls don't move when you paint their portrait. They sit still. I used Aquatec paint.

In 1977 I painted the props for *The Golden Oldies*, Dorothy Hewett's play, which was extremely potent as I could see different painted effects in the various lighting during the play and learnt a little more about how to paint shadows.

The mural in the Cosmos bookshop in St Kilda was fabulous to produce. There I was on a scaffold again, as the mural was very high and on a curved surface, well rendered by a good plasterer for me to work on. I had to think of people and books and koalas. I suppose I would regard a commission in the same way as being interviewed or filmed: you have to be alert and to the point.

14TH DECEMBER 1990   Carrillo's two erotic panels. Panels cut and one coat of Plaka Orange. Seven by two and a half feet.

Wood. Books to look at again: *Prints and Related Drawings by the Carracci Family: A Catalogue Raisonné*; *Erotic Art of the West*; *Erotic Art of the East*; *Les Amours des dieux, l'art érotique sous la renaissance, les compositions de Jules Romain, gravées par Marc-Antoine Raimondi*; a little book about classic lovemaking positions, and another which contains wondrous and phantasmagoric beings. But in the end it has to be my own style – warm colours, cadmium orange (warm, deep), flowers, wine, vines, grapes, *hommage* to Priapus, Bacchus, satyrs, nymphs, Fragonard, music, food, trees, etc.

15TH DECEMBER 1990   Second coat of red Plaka on each board. I so much want to go out and eat with a friend, Barbara Ross, to pull me away from my work. It's 12.30pm, time for a chat. I also know she is unemployed and yet has written *The Chef's Table*, a good book.

I woke up this morning and found a very scared flat mouse in my bath. First I got scared too and then I decided to get a cloth bag and I got her in it and off to the garden, where she jumped in a lemon thyme bush. I felt good all the morning because of it. Last time a mouse was in my bath I called Pompom number 1 and he took her out to the garden in his mouth. He always let them loose. Pompom number 2 eats them.

19TH DECEMBER 1990   I am well into the two panels now, faced with the mysteries of the creative process, which is life itself. The wind blows – mercifully my arse is wide open – the wind blows through the tunnels of my belly, going out through my mouth and nose, mercifully leaving my brain intact. In my little fourth volume of Diderot's *L'Encyclopédie, textes choisis les salons, préface et commentaires par* Roland Desne, I found a beautiful quotation by Vincent van Gogh: '*Je ne connais pas de meilleure définition du mot Art que celle-ci: L'art est l'homme ajouté à la nature. La Nature, la réalité, la vérité, mais avec une signifiance, avec une conception, avec un caractère que l'artiste fait ressortir et auxquels il donne de l'expression, qu'il dégage qu'il démêle affranchit, enlumine.*'

This fourth volume describes Diderot as an art critic and how he became interested in art, as he needed to include art in his encyclopaedia of the eighteenth century. It says that the word 'originality' was created in 1690, and the word 'individuality' in 1760. The time of Chardin and Vernet. Hard to imagine that the first ever exhibition of paintings occurred at the Palais Royal in 1673, the second in 1699 in the Galeries du Louvre.

I bought this adorable book in 1971 and marked it then, it is time for me to reread it. This is what happens when you pass seventy years of age. You have to reread books that gave you great pleasure and see if it works again. Knowledge is worse than lollies or chocolate or sex, it grips you and it is a road without an end.

In 1998 the National Trust allowed me to redo the bottom part of the mural at Flinders Street Station, the low relief. For many reasons, the paint I had used was peeling. It was quite an emotional few days as I had to scrape out the paint and negate colours I had put much feeling into – lucky me, the carved lines sustained me and I didn't cry too much. I held myself in distancing mode from the past. To console myself and learn more I acquired the two volumes of Italian frescoes by Steffi Roettgen, *Italian Frescoes: The Flowering of the Renaissance*, and discovered more about restoration of surviving frescoes of the Renaissance.

The new paint was especially made for architecture. The colours were very saturated. The blue was leaning towards red, the brownish red was glowing, the orange was lively – no pure red was needed as red was already in the colours I chose. It was exciting work for me to capture light with a very restricted palette and an interesting medium to use. It was the National Gallery's curator, who was also a painter, who introduced me via my son William to Keim, the paint I used, plus fixative and undercoat, ravishing to me.

At the left of the low relief I repainted the lilies light whitish-pink. The first day the scaffold had gone, I went to see the mural, very shyly. Two lovers were kissing in front of the lilies. I was right to have the lilies there and painted light white. Mission accomplished, I said to myself, and went home to study yet again a new great book on Giorgione by Jaynie Anderson, called *Giorgione: The Painter of Poetic Brevity*. On the cover of the book are a pair of androgynous eyes. I feel they are the most troubling and poignant eyes, as opposed to eyes painted of either a man or a woman, and they stare at you profoundly.

I am still thinking of the eyes on the cover of the Giorgione book. I actually know an exceptional man who has these eyes, like a gazelle's eyes when chased by a leopard and who will be caught and die. I love to be disturbed by pictures. In French you say *troublée* and it is as mysterious a way to be as life is: *sans queue ni tête*, leaving you nowhere.

But we must keep searching, learning and
loving humanity.

INSELBERGS, MOTETS AND QUODLIBETS

ike inselbergs, items rise out of my mind. My mind as a landscape.

I must be the only woman who loves washing dishes. It allows you to remember conversations you have had over the meal. You think of people who designed and made the plates of various sizes and designs. You think of the artists who worked on it. Claudia Wright came to my studio at 9 Collins Street, probably for my first interview for *Woman's Day* or *Woman's Weekly*, in 1954. She told me how she hated washing socks, and as to dishes – pooh!

In 1946 I am the protégé of Ilya Ehrenburg for six months in Paris. I go on stage at the Salle de la Mutualité and read my poem 'Hélène' (published in *Lettres françaises*). It is the time where everything happens at the Mutualité – where I have my first *valse* with my war hero, Jacques Farber; where Louis Aragon speaks and so many rare people appear. Romain Rolland in his wheelchair who wrote *Jean Christophe*, his great, well-read novel.

Melbourne 1999: when I am with young painters I can't help but search in them for my old friends of the fifties, such as Charles Blackman, John Perceval, Arthur Boyd, Cliff Pugh, and many others; also colourful and talented women. Painters are hard to compare, but David Larwill shines and others trail behind. Peter Walsh spoke to me like a real painter recently. It is hard to be a painter. Rick Amor was reading the journal of Delacroix in English; it so happened that I was reading my copy in French at the same time, there sprang a delightful conversation.

Max Delany and Simon Gregg, the curators of my retrospective at Heide, have looked at my paintings, measuring them and getting the correct titles and dates. You can never tell what a painting is about; it is often the secrets of the unconscious that one hopes to decipher privately. To be able to explain yourself you need to be asked by a poet or a writer or by Bob Sessions at Penguin.

The retrospective, at Heide at the Museum of Modern Art, is a good way to close 1999. Will I be a new painter in the next millennium? How much time have I left? And how many more books will I read before my eyes go boom-boom? Will there be no wars and bad despots? Will we turn into good human beings or will we turn into machines?

When I was young I said I would not have a retrospective in my lifetime. Now I am older I succumb. Max and Simon know my work, all the paintings and drawings. The title of the retrospective, 'Where Angels Fear to Tread', is taken from a poem by Alexander Pope. Simon has given me the book of collected poems.

A call from Julie Gibbs en route to New York. I am to write

more, so we can fill some holes. The mystery of the publisher – to construct a book. I only want to catch bits and bits – *la vie de tous les jours*.

I took out *Le Ton beau de marot* and a big silverfish fell on what I thought was my pants, but I can't feel anything so it must have gone on the floor. Douglas R. Hofstadter wrote *Le Ton beau de marot*; one could spend endless hours with such a charming writer – sailing and reading. Endless ideas like long strands of pearls, and words, words – such fun and folly.

I have to go into my Grote's *History of Greece*, written in 1856, and then Duruy's *History of Greece and of the Greek People From the Earliest Times to the Roman Conquest*, published in 1898, my big adventure. Duruy quotes Grote often, and this is how I learn about writers eyeing each other. I love the maps in these old books, and the illustrations, so tantalising in my case as my work deals with archetypal images, familiar and odd, images my subconscious nurtures. I also have the illusion that I recognise present words in ancient Greek.

I have been working on two Christmas stamps for Australia Post, on a size that will be much reduced, eliminating much detail. I am concentrating on the cones and rods in my eyes who choose and love certain colours.

Philippe is in the air coming from LA to Melbourne, Tiriel is in the air going to LA from Melbourne, and my publisher has gone to New York for two weeks. I am staying put with my book, hanging onto it by hook or by crook. So many disturbances: my retrospective at Heide has changed from John and Sunday's house number 2, which was too tumultuous in my soul and I developed a permanent *colique*. Too many memories unsolved. It is now to be in the big gallery. I always thought the dead are alive somewhere, mostly in our brain. The more one studies history and the more one fills one's brain with dead people, the more one sees that it is probably the best place to be in. The living will remember and many do.

I am also working on a painting of the Bermagui lake. My granddaughter Lily wanted to go on a little boat on the lake and so did I, but the little boat was a dinghy and had only one paddle. We pulled it along the edge of the lake where it was resting until we could attach it to the pier. It was Lily's good thinking as it was easier to go into the dinghy that way. Some friends from France arrived and kept saying, 'This is a dream.' It was: the peaceful ducks sailing, the *nénuphars* in full bloom, trees galore, and the roaring sea nearby and a sky above our head.

Suddenly I would like to read *Michelet* by Roland Barthes. Jules Michelet, *historien français né a Paris* 1798–1874, for his liberal opinions twice had his lectures suspended at the College de France. In his *Histoire de France* and *Histoire de la revolution française* Michelet succeeded in resurrecting the past. He saw woman as a minotaur: Catherine of Russia; La Duchesse d'Orléans – 'with her thick drawling speech, with her great indolence, she seemed a stagnant pool, a king of a sinister swamp'. Marie-Victoire Sophie de Noailles, pious, sugary, still fresh, plump and lovely – this lady had the privilege of reassuring and even attracting a very timid king. No need for Viagra in those days.

When I finish reading my Grote *et* Duruy, I think I will read Michelet's *Histoire de la revolution française*. Victor Hugo loved his *Histoire de France*. I wish, I wish.

In France, when you go to school the first history sentence is: '*Il y a 2000 ans, nôtre pays s'appelait la Gaule et ses habitants, les Gaulois*'. One is about a seven-year-old child and one never forgets this little sentence. As a child, Charlemagne was my hero, as we were taught that he would show people how to read and write sitting under a large oak tree.

I find a typed letter my husband wrote in Paris:

26th December 1950

N. Slezak esq.
C/- Socomin Ltd
473–481 Bourke Street
Melbourne C.1

Dear Mr Slezak,

Thank you very much for your letter of the 12th inst.

We are extremely happy that our application has been accepted and we are very grateful for your help.

My last cable was a consequence of war hysteria over the world.

When ready with visas and so on, we shall take the airplane via New York–San Francisco–Sydney. Have you something to do for Socomin in New York?

I noted your new line of building materials, however, I would like to have your reply on my letter of the 21st of November.

Evidently my English has to be brushed up, but I think two or three months business activity in the country will be the best way. However, I have taken some lessons for two months.

Mrs Mora is prepared to do all housework, 'hard labour', personally *pour l'amour de son mari* (hm-hum). Anyhow she is an artist . . .

My best regard to Mrs Slezak.

Yours truly,

Georges Mora

And there we are, history, 1950, and how to catch history? I know Professor Weston Bate, who is a historian. He has written many books; painters and historians are not unalike, they deal with time and facts and all the same are poets, like Geoffrey Dutton, like Professor Geoffrey Bolton. They are writers and possessed. They know people very well, and they sculpt time.

Slowly I see the ink going low in my ink bottles; ink into pen, into words, into my exercise books, to make a book, to make a book, to make a book. Long ago, at school, it was terrible to punish children and make them write a phrase a hundred times. In Romania my mother, when punished at school, circa 1904, would be made to stand in a corner with her shoes full of hard beans. In France I remember *le bonnet d'âne* – a large hat with donkey's ears – and also being told to stand in a corner of the classroom.

As usual, as I write, my cat Pompom purrs, sitting on the back of me, on my chair. Today he looks a very large cat as he ate, in its entirety, a most beautiful black, furry, shiny rat. For one instant, in the moonlight reflecting on the fur, I thought I could make some good painting brushes, but Pompom gobbled it all up.

Deborah Hart, a well-known art historian, is coming to interview me for *Art in Australia*. Nothing is better than a brilliant interviewer; you have to let your wild brain loose and hope to catch pearls and enrich everyone, and maybe discover your work a little more closely.

In the meantime, the insanity of Kosovo continues and it is hard to live through this terrible fight against one man who repeats history at its worse. But he must lose as people's humanity always wins in the end – alas with many innocent people and courageous people paying with their lives. Suddenly I find myself writing a poem:

Nothing is sadder
than landscapes
through a war,
skies and rivers
through a war.
Flowers, autumn and spring,
summer and winter.
Empty towns with their
schools empty of children.
Their cafés empty of people
and the cemeteries perplexed
in summer.

Watching *Australian Story* on the ABC. 'The Long Day's Task' follows the epic journey of five new Care Australia volunteers from Sydney to Macedonia. Good people facing the hopelessness of children, mothers, fathers, old people arriving in buses at night uncovered in my brain the hidden pain of having experienced arrival in the camp de Pithiviers and also three days and three nights at the Vélodrome d'Hiver on 16th July 1942 in Paris. I suddenly cry terribly, sobbing, letting go. I fear convulsive gasps, and the show on TV ends, thankfully. I feel very wounded as one does not know really how the brain works. But I am grateful to my brain for recognising moments it had previously stamped out of my mind, probably to protect itself.

My friend Neilma has gone to Paris, Maine. She loves Paris anywhere in the world, in Texas, in France. My friend and her mother eat a most delicious lobster in Paris, Maine.

Looking at photographs in a Paris drawing book I had assembled of Saint-Quay-Portrieux and the three belles of Georges Mora. Georges, Philippe and me in Paris, baby in my arms, facing the world. Our voyages through France before leaving for Australia. McKinnon. Melbourne. Photos of our wedding taken three weeks after the wedding. Engagement photos. Family photos. Letters. Notes. Lists of fabulous people I have met passing by or living in Melbourne.

Last night, listening to Kerouac, Burroughs' writings and voices, I suddenly looked at my two wrists and realised how easy it would be to end one's life, with lots of champagne of course. Beware of one's quirky brain, I said to myself.

Photos of Georges in Hyères in an OSE *maison d'enfants*, 1942. Stunning letter from 1945 by Georges Garel, hero of the Resistance, describing Georges Mora, Chef de Bureau. Photos of me at Ecole d'Education Par le Jeu et l'Art Dramatique in Paris, and at Pau in the Basses Pyrénées. Letter from my father telling me not to send money to Israel. I had sent him twenty-five dollars.

I remember my friend Neilma telling me about sitting down talking to her sister Marigold, and noticing her sister's likeness to their mother, Dame Merlyn Myer. I wonder where the two sisters were; what time, what light, what mood causes those we've loved and have lost to reappear in our mind and make everything transient, allowing poems to be born, or gentle prose dare to appear.

Last Sunday, 25th April 1999, Arthur Boyd died at the Mercy Hospital, Melbourne. I cry. Last time I saw Arthur was at my son William's Windsor Place gallery. Arthur hugged me and no words were necessary. He came to buy a painting. I grieve deeply, he was such a nice man and a great painter, too young to die at seventy-eight. I loved his mother, and listened to his father's ideas many a time in the fifties as he showed me his pencil-coloured drawings in exercise books. He was so absent-minded, it was rare to be by his side. Arthur's mother Doris was graceful, and a lovely watercolourist too.

I grieve and suddenly remember that I didn't grieve enough for my mother, as she died one week after my father's death, interrupting my grieving for my father. I am howling so hard, so hard that I stop, thinking I could choke and die. It is twenty years ago now and it feels like ten years ago. Michelet comes back into my head, his idea of people, and goodness and education for the people. His ideas of the brain, who is male and female.

Talking to grandchildren far away, unable to put the phone down and cut the thread.

I wonder what one thinks just before dying, or does one just smile? Some people scream, some lose their breath. I have an odd book called *Death and Sudden Death* by P. Brouardel and F. Lucas Benham. P. Brouardel was Professor of Medical Jurisprudence, and Dean of the Faculty of Medicine in Paris. F. Lucas Benham was a Member of the Royal College of Physicians of London. How curious, the birth of a book. The preface to the second edition was written by F. Lucas Benham in Exeter, South Australia, 1902. The translator's preface is also by F. Lucas Benham, 1896. The peculiar subject of the book is the danger of premature burial and the unforeseen nature of sudden death, which have occupied public attention for all time. The causes of sudden death are but ill understood. They are very numerous; they often cause the suggestion of crime or suicide to be raised, and give rise to medico-legal inquiries.

Dear reader, if you will forgive me, I shall write down some of the contents of the book. I do have sometimes a most peculiar sense of humour and I excuse myself. Here it goes:

PART I THE SIGNS OF DEATH
CHAPTER I The Moment of Death: Apparent Death
CHAPTER II The Uncertainty of the Signs of Death, and Premature Burial
CHAPTER III The Signs of Death
CHAPTER IV Rigor Mortis
CHAPTER V Putrefaction
CHAPTER VI Cremation: Mummification
CHAPTER VII Legislation, Medico-Legal Applications

I am starting to tremble and can't go on to Part II, Chapter XIII, where I see 'Sudden Death in Children: Intestinal Disorders'.

I am scared, but one must know. Part II, Chapter IV is 'Sudden Death Due to Lesions of The Repiratory System: Compression of the Chest – Tight Lacing'. All the pretty girls who thought they fainted with love were just tight-laced, on their pretty waists. I did it myself in the fifties, wearing a *guêpière*, fainting often. There are many nineteenth-century novels with girls fainting in church, their stays being too tight. Many cases are quoted in *Death and Sudden Death* in the various lectures to gentlemen doctors, as in those days women were not doctors, or could not practise. The gentlemen are told to get older maids in order not to be accused of bad behaviour if young maids die of extra-uterine gestation:

> Gentlemen, you are young; allow me to give you a piece of advice: when a physician is young and unmarried, he ought only to take into his service females who are plain and who have passed the canonical age.

And from page 201 in *Death and Sudden Death*, this story:

> Sudden death from emotion is a stock incident with writers of romance; unfortunately, these almost always belong in every sense to fiction and have no claim whatever to science. It is important, moreover, to separate myth from fact in all such cases which occur in real life.
>
> All varieties of emotion are capable of inducing sudden death.
>
> One of the most striking instances of sudden death from horror is narrated in the Memoir of the Sansons. At an execution in Paris on August 19, 1792, in the early days of the guillotine, a beardless young man, who wore the red

cap, came forward and, mainly out of curiosity, volunteered his assistance. Sanson, the head executioner, being short-handed, took him at his word, made him ascend the scaffold, and gave him the cord to pull which liberated the knife, 'in order that he might display his patriotism.' He then directed him to pick up the severed head and exhibit it to the crowd. 'He took the head by the hair and advanced to the edge of the scaffold; but, as he was raising his arm to show the bloody trophy, he staggered and fell back. M. Sanson came to his assistance, thinking that he was fainting; but he discovered that he was dead. Violent emotion had brought on an apoplectic fit, which killed him instantaneously.'

Another story I love comes from page 203:

A man living in India was roused from sleep by feeling something creeping over his naked legs. He had an innate horror of reptiles, and fancied it was a cobra. He became collapsed and died in six hours, though it was found before his death that the reptile was only a harmless lizard.

And one of my favourite stories, also on page 203:

A lady of quality, who in the year 1681 had several times seen without alarm the wonderful comet which then appeared, was one night tempted to examine it by means of a telescope; the sight of it, however, in this way terrified her so much that she was with difficulty carried safely home, and, the impression remaining, she died a few days afterwards.

Ah! What a charming book I am reading. I always thought that doctors would be good story writers, they have the imagery and *surprises visuelles et psychologiques* at their fingertips (a pun). They have to think like detectives of the body and the brain. I am getting more and more scared to read the book in case my body recognises something dangerous and I will die a sudden death. But knowledge is an expensive pleasure and I shall peruse the book just a little longer.

The word 'adipocere', a greyish waxy substance formed by the decomposition of soft tissues in dead bodies subjected to moisture, origin nineteenth-century, from the French *adipocire*, from Latin *adeps adipis*, fat; plus French *cire*, wax, from Latin *cera*. One can, and I do, spend hours finding the etymology of a word. I think in Brouardel's book I love best the passages on putrefaction. It is vile, and please forgive me: the attraction is because I am an optimist, and the body makes a lot of noises and therefore explodes and protests a little longer. Sometimes it transforms itself into armies of mites if the coffin is open.

I could go into the various qualities of coffins and cemeteries that preserve you or destroy you – it's a bit like knowing good terrain for growing vines – but page 92 of *Death and Sudden Death* is calling me and I read 'of all the organs, the uterus putrefies last; for a long time after death its examination is capable of affording precise information'.

Another story I have heard: the body of a servant girl, eighteen years of age, was found at the bottom of a well. She was buried, but after more than a year had gone by, her master was suspected of having caused her to become pregnant and thrown her into the well, and he was arrested in consequence; however, he denied it strenuously. An exhumation was ordered and a doctor was appointed to undertake investigation. The uterus, eighteen months after burial, had still the shape of one that had never been impregnated. The accused man naturally was acquitted.

I am sure that lectures given now to students of medicine with the aid of computers must be stunning – well, what is more haunting, the image or the word? Maybe each is as haunting as the other. I have to say that, being a maker of images but loving words dementedly, the word 'Dharuk' comes to mind, an Aboriginal language in the area of Sydney, now spoken rarely. Ah! But the word 'Dharuk' exists and is handsome, and sounds of it evoke a strange, long-ago time, when we had to walk for a living instead of work for a living.

After a phone call from a friend, I must, will, am reading Alexander Pope and when I arrive at line 625 there is 'where angels fear to tread'. It is a long journey with Alexander Pope, and, as my mother would say, art gives life. Two lines I love: 'Thus in the soul while memory prevails/the solid power of understanding fails'.

Sitting in the sun at the Café Deveroli in Acland Street, where a great mime is all painted in white and moving so slowly when people put money in his cup. Watching him, I cry, as this great artist brings back to me *les rues de Paris* of my childhood.

This live sculpture brings art into the street at its highest degree. Children especially are mesmerised. His eyes look like glass as his lids are painted white. He sends kisses to the ladies who put money in his cup and shakes hands with the men, his hands in white gloves. His stillness is *magique* and the slowness of his movements sheer poetry. When I first walked past him, I thought it was a sculpture, then remembered art. Imagine, all the morning I was thinking about art, writing to Deborah Hart whose perception of my art is quite uncanny (meeting her is like meeting Hephzibah Menuhin, a sister in Art), and there I am in the street passing and being lured from my thoughts about what credit is in my cheque book. I passed art for a split second and stopped, realising what pleasure I was almost missing.

Half an hour has passed and I am still watching the white sculptured man and I see him cough. He stands up, slightly bending over, descends from his pedestal to exercise his legs, and now is back in his position on the white pedestal, his two arms slightly bent, like a doll's, his back leaning forward.

It is amazing to see how simple and poor people give him money, more than sophisticated people who are passing by. It is pure theatre in the street. He wears a white jolly hat with a short edge. He gives lollies to children after calling them with his right index finger; for a beautiful girl, he took something dark from the inside of his vest, maybe a dried flower, to give to her.

My schooling with Marcel Marceau awakes more sensitivity in my thoughts and movements as I watch this beautiful mime in Acland Street, Melbourne, 1999. In our fast times it is amazing that people stop and are seduced by the stillness of this artist.

I have gone back to tenth- and eleventh-century manuscripts for the Christmas stamps I have to design for Australia Post. A big interruption in my writing, making two designs for Australia Post. Thinking of the picture: its colours and its reduced size. I have *The*

Illuminated Book: Its History and Production, by David Diringer. A rare book I bought in 1958 at F.W. Cheshire in Little Collins Street. A fabulous bookshop who has gone forever now, also its owner Mr Fabinyi. If I may say that, I always have had a good instinct for rare books and always managed to find the money to buy them and often no money for food. To soothe my stomach so hungry, I would go to bed with a good cooking book and read recipes. One book I remember especially was *L'Art culinaire moderne* by Henri-Paul Pellaprat, with a preface by Curnonsky, *prince élu des gastonomes, président-fondateur de l'Académie des Gastronomes*. The perfect book for hungry and artistic people.

Maybe I will tell Pasiphaë's story now. It is one of my favourites. Pasiphaë falls in love with the divine bull that Poseidon has offered to her husband King Minos. Pasiphaë goes to see the inventor Daedalus. She will ask Daedalus to build a mechanical cow where she can fit in, lodge in. The idea is so ingenious that the bull thinks it is a real cow and introduces his *fascinum* in Pasiphaë's vulva. She at last can enjoy *la volupté* of the beast (*ferinas voluptates*). In my *Oxford Classical Dictionary* it says that Minos was so furious that he emprisoned Daedalus, who escaped later of course. The Pasiphaë story I so love is from *Le Sexe et l'effroi*, by Pascal Quignard.

Watching football last night with the Crows and the Tigers and the rain made me think of Botticelli's paintings for Dante's *Inferno*. The rain made the ball slippery. The Tigers (Richmond) won and it was all embrace, paradise, the rain already falling on the happy faces. I dare not tell that I was in bed already, listening to the game on the radio, but the last quarter of the game and the rain and the excitement made me go out to the TV room and I watched entranced, leaving the radio on as well.

Four weeks at Wesley Primary School, painting with children, watching all the young mothers and all the teachers and Kim Anderson, the principal of the school. The boys who wanted to paint the forest we are creating as if it was on fire. No sooner did my head turn than the two boys painted magic red fires, but this was not the idea; the idea was to paint a forest with trees of all sizes and shapes and its inhabitants. The boys, not giving up, asked if they could paint red trees. Not on, and we parted company laughing. The boys painted therefore little black trees, as this week we only use the colour black. Next week it will be white and then yellow and a colour the children desire. The students see every week their work getting more strength, transforming itself: they are puzzled.

The moon in my little binoculars looked so luminous last night. There was also in the sky a red star and a blue star. My heartbeat kept my binoculars moving, and the stars looked like worms in the sky: *vers luisants*, glow-worms. I miss my telescope I gave to one of my children, who left it one night on his balcony. Next morning we realised someone had climbed up the balcony and stolen the telescope. I kept thinking of the lady of quality in the seventeenth century who dies after looking at a comet in her telescope; I could well imagine it happening as I was drinking with my eyes the moon looking so extraordinarily lonely there in the universe. 'The sky is full of rocks,' I remember reading in my dictionary description of the sky, a seventeenth-century French dictionary: *Le Furetière*. So, we are in danger all the time.

Today is Sunday. The day when one should go promenading, meeting friends. My friends are my books and I realise I have not read yet *Somebody Else* by Charles Nicholl, which is about Arthur Rimbaud in Africa. '*Je est un autre*,' Arthur Rimbaud wrote in *Lettre du Voyant*. I often think of *Je est un autre*. We are always someone else and the great search is to find one's real self, at one's peril, and hopefully to grow into a better being.

A book by Patricia Dobrez has arrived, a large book, *Michael Dransfield's Lives: A Sixties Biography*, the story of a poet who died at twenty-three. He loved drugs and wanted to give them up, but fate had another scenario and Michael Dransfield died in a mysterious way: such is life for the brave sometimes. So I cry and turn to reading poetry when I am in strife: nineteenth-century poetry, American poems, Australian poems, French poems, Japanese poems of women 'languishing', English poems. A poem is a good anchor to help you go back to life and work: in my case, painting, as I do not paint if my sadness overcomes my soul. That is when I play with my toys to pass the time, or go into the kitchen and cook dishes *à la française*: very homely and tasty and simple, with good ingredients of course, and butter and garlic and *échalotes* and fine herbs and wine and fresh cream, fresh eggs. And I am ready to do an *omelette à la Parisienne* with Sauce Bercy.

Suddenly, I think of all the chefs who worked at the Balzac and Tolarno restaurants. I miss them very much. It was nice to discuss dishes – it was not necessary to follow fashion, but moods – and to remember the history of famous dishes. I have been reading an article called '*Cuisine et société*' in *Le Figaro*, 23rd December 1999, a fine lesson to ponder. Mothers as cooks are disappearing as the social role of the chef grows. And beware, painters, as chefs become artists!

My father loved 'grog', which is a popular drink in Paris on a cold day. Put a good measure of pale rum in a tumbler, add a teaspoon of sugar, three cloves and a wedge of lemon. Top up with boiling water and stir well.

I remember my mother's springtime dish, a *jardinière* I have not been able to recreate. I remember Paulette's roast pork with endive. I remember horse meat – *viande hachée* thrown in a bouillon, the meat raw I had to eat quickly to grow up in good health. Needless to say, the horse's head on the door of the butcher's shop was very unsettling. I had to eat chicken wings in order to fly, the crest of the rooster in order to be clever. The bones with *moëlle* my father loved. The marrow always made my father sing opera excerpts and we were all happy. My mother and her sisters made magic walnut cakes on Saturday afternoons; I have described this in a little book called *Too Many Walnuts: Jewish Cooking, Jewish Cooks* by Ramona Koval. When I was a good girl, Mother would let me bite into the butter, especially if mice had been at it, to make my teeth stronger. Growing up in Paris was heaven for children, looking at the *pâtisseries*, lolly shops, chocolate shops. The lollies of many colours still roll in my head, they were so pretty and tasted fruity.

I am about to face the biggest adventure of all, that of aging gracefully. There will be fun and games as I feel old age is like adolescence – your body changes and all is possible learning-wise, even though one has a funny way of getting up from a seat and waiting for your legs to start walking; even though your bladder leaks and all array of pads are on offer, thin ones, winged ones, pink, white and blue. The best is your memory tricking you day-wise: is it Sunday or Monday? A rest in the afternoon, one wakes up, is it morning or evening? Things disappear and you always find them again right in front of you. Books to read three or four pages at a time, and patience is de rigeur as I have to keep my eyes for my painting, my watercolours, my pastels. Soft dolls are too hard to make for my hands now, I miss creating them terribly. I miss my embroideries, but with big needles one can make very nice French knots. I call them love knots. And one can flirt, of course, knowing with age '*le Jeu de l'amour at du hasard*' (Pierre de Marivaux). As I say, one can choose one's pleasures and miseries and all is well, but I hear Dylan Thomas – do not go gentle into that good night. But life goes on till the last minutes and should I read now letters of great painters or more recipes like *vol-au-vent à la financière* I love so much, or should I listen to Lully? My cat Pompom needs fresh food and does not like tinned food and stares at me. I think of all my grandchildren who have a little bit of me to face their lives, and I think of all my ancestors who survived so I could also. Oh! To understand time either through your ancestors or through your descendants, both ways as puzzling as the mystery of the brain, the mystery of art, of imagination, of innocence, the universe. I am grateful to be alive; even so, old age knocks at my door and a funny visitor it is.

I danced with a bad leg, a Panadol, three glasses of champagne, two of red wine and one vodka, and as the music started I passed out for a split second. My partner rescued me and I cannot remember who it was. I who love dancing so much had to realise that a bad leg is not an obedient tool.

The joy of dancing. Four beautiful men I danced with, their names in my *carnet de bal*, then I returned to my table where

Mr G. Whitlam was sitting alone. Mr Gough Whitlam of course knew my two friends Victor Duruy and George Grote, who each wrote the history of ancient Greece. The dancing party was to celebrate the hundredth birthday of Sydney Myer.

My retrospective is shaping itself with curators and photographers and paintings and drawings and dolls, all quite bewildering, and media I love. *Objets inanimés, avez-vous donc une âme?* Yes, paintings, artwork have a soul and the mystery grows. Psychologically, this show of my fifty years of art really puts me upside down and causes me pains right through my body, and even my brain joins the brouhaha – a French word turned English.

Time for me to disappear in one of my favourite books, *Curiosities of Literature* by Isaac D'Israeli. The index itself, in the following order, is such a delight:

Abelard, unjust condemnation of, 55

Actors who have fallen martyrs to their
tragic *caractères*, 94

Addison, deficient in conversation, 40

Alberico, his visions, the source of Dante's
Inferno, 334

Ancestors, their different modes of
life, 253

Angels, scholastic disquisitions on, 23

Aquinas, Thomas
the scholastic divine, 23
his disquisition on Angels, 23–24

Apuleius, an ingenious thought of, 27

This beautiful index is a kind of orgy of the mind. I want to read it all, but it would take time off my painting, my autobiography, my life.

Max Delany is coming to discuss his writing for the catalogue with me; he knows my work so well, I am sure it will be perfect. One can't go far enough into one's work, perhaps someone else can. I remember being at the Phillip's Institute and sitting next to Peter Fuller, whose brilliance I could fathom, but the handling of his words and erudition left me like a stunned mullet. Poor man died in a sudden death a year later, 1990. I will be listening to Max Delany very carefully and will be very honoured to do so.

André Gide: A Life in the Present, by Alan Sheridan, is waiting for me to read. My friend Genevieve rang Cosmos bookshop to ask which book I would love. Sophie, who works there and who lent me her Greek grammar books when I was studying Greek, remembered that I was lusting after Gide but, having big debts at the bookshop, I resisted buying it, which is unlike me. I have many works by Gide in French, who had made a big impression on me *avec son L'Immoraliste*, his journal of 1939–1949. Many of his books and plays we would devour in Paris, Georges and myself, and our literary friends.

L'Immoraliste contains unrequited love, one of my favourite subjects. Men are so puzzling, I thought as a young girl, and still do, and women are wild at any age.

I am creating a little tableau of a tea party, cakes and cups and tea set from my doll's house; strange personages such as a snake-lady, a little doll with my own hair, three funny little animals sitting on a long chair, a paper doll, a cat on a *trottinette* – he is pink and the *trottinette* blue.

How long can I stay in a quodlibetical mood? It must be the word, its sound, its look, that captured my fancy. I also remember I have to read a lovely book on cod fishing, maybe this is the reason. *Cod: A Biography of the Fish that Changed the World*, by Mark Kurlansky: the cover of the book promises a truly special read. Sea at the top, big wave, codfish, name of writer, *sans majuscules* – that is, no capital letters – and at the bottom of the cover three fishermen each holding a cod with mouth wide open.

And next to my cod book, waiting also to be read, is Stefan Gabanyi's *Whisk(e)y*. When I reach eighty-five years, I want to be very knowledgeable about fine whiskey – very hard to switch from fine cognacs one grew up with as a young *femme*. The one I bought recently to 'study', Talisker, from the Isle of Skye, inspired me no end, but I will try to wait until the right age. I am still in the champagne craze, oh happy guzzle habit.

Betty Churcher opened my exhibition with a very thorough appreciation of my work. I was very moved. My three sons were there, three grandchildren and my *belle-fille* Lucy also. The exhibition has attracted endless waves of people and sobers me up and I am very honoured to give much pleasure to so many people.

One young woman thought the show was sad. I pointed out that it is much about tenderness – fancy mixing up sadness and tenderness. Maybe she was right. I have to investigate the word 'tenderness' from all angles. I was puzzled by my answer. To be young is too soon to be sad. So what is tenderness? In my case it is the love I have for people who suffer uselessly.

Soon the retrospective will leave the walls and works will
return to their respective owners. As for me, after falling to the
bottom of the sea, by now I am a little cork floating on
the crest of a wave, slowly feeling yet again
wicked and virtuous.

epilogue: MY House IN Barkly Street

hen I learnt and comprehended that I was to leave Barkly Street, I felt like a snake leaving its skin in the summer, like the Christmas beetle gripping still a little longer on the tree bark. It is hard to leave a place at any time of your life; it is your memories *entassées* that you have to leave behind, but they will attach themselves to you.

Number 116 Barkly Street is an Edwardian house built circa 1890. I fell in love with it as it had a wood stove, which I used twice in twenty years. It warmed the house and made a lovely noise. The two fireplaces with lovely tiles and mirror above the mantelpiece I also used rarely. The little pantry I dreamt to stock with food was soon stocked with books and photo albums, chess boards, suitcases. My beloved little kitchen is really the bathroom. The bathtub resides in the garden and a shower was built in its place, very old Paris way.

Springtime has appeared in the garden, the trees are in flower, and the avocado tree has so many fruits and flowers again. Next springtime I will be in Tanner Street, Richmond, in a building created by Chris De Campo, the architect. On the first floor, William Mora Galleries and my studio, *et le ciel par-dessus le toit* . . . Pompom and I will have a balcony to share. I dare not tell the trees that we are leaving, but the little garden knows. One must always leave. To return is harder.

Ma chambre at Barkly Street is the end room; from its window I see trees and hear birds early in the morning, and kitty loves coming in through the window. Following the front room is my writing room, who was once my embroidery room. I painted twice in it: a large work, the erotic two panels. In the front room I painted *Ghosts* for the Malthouse Theatre, but my favourite place to paint is the wood-stove room attached to the pantry.

In the *petit jardin* I painted several times. Painting outside changes your style, but nice sometimes to obey nature. I painted potplants, the cat next door on the fence with the red house bricks behind. I painted the plaster angel but destroyed the painting; I have a photo of it.

The nectarine tree has grown large and made my neighbours and birds very happy. My avocado tree makes the possums happy, and me and friends. A garden has its own secrets, and the dreams I had on the swinging chaise longue when I tried impatiently to rest. The jasmine plant a painter brought me once grew all over and perfumed the thoughts floating about. *Mad Dog Morgan* films and materials also reside in the garden shed with my bike and scooter, and I am faced with discarding many things as a studio has other demands than a house: wardrobe or toys? Off with the wardrobe. Shelves built in the studio for books: off with the bookcases. I have to gear myself right through my brain for going to a beautiful new abode. I have insisted on having the bathtub outside the bathroom, and the walls of the bathroom semitransparent so I can enjoy my bidet from every angle of the studio.

One hot summer afternoon at Barkly Street, the kind when you should be making love, I was alone, so I decided to dig alongside the house. I found a little bakelite doll's arm. I thought if there was a girl's toy, there could also be a boy's toy, so I dug a little deeper and found a toy soldier on a lead horse. I said to myself, if there were children, there might be traces of parents, so I dug a bit further and found a diamanté brooch, and I kept digging and found little medicine glass bottles, and I kept digging, by then sweating like a teacup. I found a soldier's insignia, the sort attached to hats I had seen many times in pictures. I found bits of lovely thick decorated porcelain, and the afternoon passed quickly. I thought of the long-ago previous owners of Barkly Street. I also found in a little cellar an enamelled 1920s *bassine* which made me happy and helped me to date the other objects. I planned to dig more another time, but the mood did not return.

I have never listened to reason and have had a bumpy ride, and survived desperately looking for wisdom as reason is incomprehensible to me. It is too abstract, too complicated; the logic of reason baffles me and maybe there isn't any. All the same, I have always protected my work, my free spirit, and remain independent and poor in my old age, ready to tackle death my way. How? I am thinking about it and it better be good, maybe a big party and filmed while I say goodbye and thank you. I have a beautiful enormous book written by Michel Vovelle in 1983. Its title: *La Mort et l'occident de 1300 à nos jours*. I think I will have fun rereading it and prepare myself with style.

Nouzette told me once about paradise, purgatory and hell, and the devil with his fork waiting to catch you. For a long time in Paris as a child, I imagined the devil and his fork at the door of lifts and I was petrified, thinking the lift would descend right down to hell. By the age of ten, I thought more of purgatory, and had many nightmares about it as I saw Dante's *Inferno* painted by Botticelli, which my father had introduced me to. As I grew up slightly my thoughts leant towards paradise with many angels everywhere. Now that the time of death approaches, I roam through the universe as a little bit of dust looking to plant myself in a star and grow again one day somewhere. Lady Casey once told me that dust is nourishing. There lies a mystery, unfathomable.

Letter to My Womb, 1928-1993

13th August 1998

When you appear in my painting
in the shape of a bird's body, I
say hello. But you have no right
to appear without warning me.

Usually I destroy the painting.
Today I shall keep you, as almost
six years have passed since
you were invaded by cancer via
the cervix we shared. I face the
phantom womb who keeps appearing in my work. You still have
an enormous power over me as you
were the little house of my three
children, also a trap — my being
on heat every four years, wanting
a child at any price, with sex. It
is uncanny how you appear and
I know it is you, my womb, the

shape of a pear, with horns
(Fallopian tubes). It is eerie
to recognise a part of oneself that
one has never seen. A bit like
a lover, you are.

I love receiving oracles in my drawings
or paintings, but your message is too
close to home. It unsettles me. You
stare at me. You have been sliced to
be studied; your presence is for ever
haunting me.
We have had good times. Remember
when Dr. K. thought you had twins
and I prepared two sets of layettes
and two bassinets but only one baby
came out? You are a trick, you are.
Remember I loved you when you
shaped my body when I was 20, 25, 30
years old. I still love you in your phan-
-tom shape. I didn't think I would ever
write you a letter after almost six
years of parting from each other.

It is like writing a letter to a dead lover, like Dear Spence, which I read in Me: Stories of my Life by Katherine Hepburn. She was a great actor, and lover too. It was Professor Geoffrey Bolton who told me to read her book. You can always be at ease with dead lovers or dead wombs, you can't hear them. They are like snow, without a voice, as Sylvia Plath said.

Sometimes I think a new womb could grow in my tummy but nature is not that smart. Who knows? The charming doctor who came to visit me with his mother as I was working on a mosaic project in St. Kilda is the doctor who invented the clamp, an instrument to hold the womb as it was taken out. Dear Womb, I often have that image in my mind of when you left — held by the pincer, the clamp. I miss you, my womb, but am grateful to have some more life left, thanks to Professor Michael Quinn and all the nurses and surgeons. I wonder how you looked, probably covered with blood to give me more life.

so we have parted and you are kind to appear sometimes and say hello. I never know when I will see you. Today you appeared on the shoulder of a young girl. I have caught you in several line drawings but closed the drawing book after seeing you. Maybe I shall be kinder to your apparitions and let you be in any form you want to be from now on. But you are uncanny, you never change your shape so I can recognise you at once, and I often become distraught, like a lost lover whose questions are never answered. I can't hear you, only see you, and have to let you go to your wanderings in my magic subconscious. Thank You, Dr Freud.

LiST OF BOOKS iN THe TeXT

Abélard and Héloïse, *Lettres complètes d'Abélard et d'Héloïse*, Librairie Garnier
    Frères, Paris

Acts of the Twentieth International Congress of the History of Art, *Studies in
    Western Art* (4 vols), Princeton University Press, Princeton, 1963

Alain-Fournier, *Le Grand Meaulnes*, Emile-Paul Frères, Paris, 1967

Alvarez, Al, *The Savage God: A Study of Suicide*, Weidenfeld & Nicolson,
    London, 1971

Andahazi, Federico, *The Anatomist*, trans. Alberto Manguel, Anchor,
    Sydney, 1998

Anderson, Jaynie, *Giorgione: The Painter of Poetic Brevity*, Flammarion,
    New York, 1997

Apollinaire, Guillaume, *Ouevres poétiques*, Gallimard, Paris, 1956

Atget, Eugène, *Paris*, Gingko Press, Santa Rosa, 1993

Bail, Murray, *Eucalyptus*, Text Publishing, Melbourne, 1998

Barthes, Roland, *La Chambre claire: Note sur la photographie*, Gallimard Seuill, Paris, 1980

——*Michelet*, Editions du Seuil, Paris, 1954

Berenson, Bernard, *Lorenzo Lotto*, Phaidon Press, London, 1956

Berlin, Brent and Kay, Paul, *Basic Color Terms, Their Universality and Evolution*, University of California Press, Berkeley, 1969

Bingham, Colin, *The Affairs of Women: A Modern Miscellany*, Currawong, Sydney, 1969

Blanc, Charles, *Grammaire des arts du dessin*, Renouards, Paris, 1880

Bohlin, Diane DeGrazia, *Prints and Related Drawings by the Carracci Family: A Catalogue Raisonné*, National Gallery of Art, Washington, 1979

Boldrewood, Rolf, *Old Melbourne Memories*, George Robertson, Melbourne, 1884

Botticelli, Sandro, *Drawings for Dante's Inferno*, Lear, New York, 1947

Brady, E. J., *Australia Unlimited*, Robertson, Melbourne, 1918

Brouardel, P. and Benham, F. Lucas, *Death and Sudden Death*, Baillière, Tindall and Cox, London, 1902

Camus, Albert, *L'Eté*, Gallimard, Paris 1954

——*L'Etranger*, Gallimard, Paris, 1957

——*La Chute*, Gallimard, Paris, 1956

——*La Peste*, Gallimard, Paris, 1947

——*Le Mythe de Sisyphe*, Gallimard, Paris, 1942

——*Noces,* Gallimard, Paris, 1959

Ciano, Galeazzo Conte, *Journal politique* (2 vols), La Presse Française et Etrangère, Paris, 1947

Clarke, John R., *Looking at Lovemaking: Constructions of Sexuality in Roman Art, 100BC–AD250*, University of California Press, Berkeley, 1998

Clune, Frank, *Dig: A Drama of Central Australia*, Angus & Robertson, Sydney, 1965

Colette, *Cheri*, Fayard, Paris, 1928

——*Douze dialogues de bêtes*, Gallimard, Paris, 1932

Crossland, Robert, *Wainewright in Tasmania*, Oxford University Press, Melbourne, 1954

de Beauvoir, Simone, *Beloved Chicago Man: Letters to Nelson Algren*, Gollancz, London, 1998

——*Le Deuxième Sexe,* Gallimard, Paris, 1949

——*Le Sang des autres*, Gallimard, Paris, 1945

Delacroix, Eugène, *Journal d'Eugène Delacroix* (3 vols), Plon, Paris, 1932

Diderot, Denis, *L'Encyclopédie*, Pergamon Press, Paris, 1966

Diringer, David, *The Illuminated Book: Its History and Production*, Faber, London, 1967

D'Israeli, Isaac, *Curiosities of Literature*, George Routledge and Sons, London, 1889

Dobrez, Patricia, *Michael Dransfield's Lives: A Sixties Biography*, Melbourne University Press, Melbourne, 1999

Doxiadis, Euphrosyne, *The Mysterious Fayum Portraits: Faces from Ancient Egypt*, H. N. Abrams, New York, 1995

Dunand, Louis and Lemarchand, Philippe, *Les Amours des dieux* (3 vols), Instit d'Iconographie Arietis, Lausanne, 1977

Duruy, Victor, *History of Greece and of the Greek People From the Earliest Times to the Roman Conquest* (4 vols), trans. M.M. Ripley, Kegan Paul, Trench, Trübner & Co., London, 1898

Faguet, Emile, *La Prose française: Extraits de tous les Auteurs*, Librairie des Annales, Paris, 1912

Fauchery, Antoine, *Sun Pictures of Victoria: The Fauchery–Daintree Collection, 1858*, Currey O'Neil Ross, Melbourne, 1983

Flaubert, Gustave, *La Tentation de Saint Antoine*, Gallimard, Paris, 1983

——*Correspondance* (2 vols), Gallimard, Paris, 1973

Furetière, Antoine, *Le Dictionnaire universel* (2 vols), Le Robert, Paris, 1978

Gabanyi, Stefan, *Whisk(e)y*, Abbeville Press, New York, 1997

Gage, John, *Colour and Culture: Practice and Meaning from Antiquity to Abstraction*, Thames and Hudson, London, 1993

Gide, André, *L'Immoraliste*, Mercvre de France, Paris, 1957

Gowing, Lawrence, *Paintings in the Louvre*, Stewart, Tabori & Chang, New York, 1987

Grote, George, *History of Greece* (12 vols), Dent, London, 1906

Hammond, N.G.L. and Scullard, H.H. (eds), *The Oxford Classical Dictionary*, Clarendon Press, Oxford, 1970

Harding, M. Esther, *The Way of All Women: A Psychological Interpretation*, Rider, London, 1971

Harris, Max, *The Vegetative Eye*, Reed and Harris, Melbourne, 1943

Hepburn, Katherine, *Me: Stories of My Life*, Penguin, London, 1992

Hofstadter, Douglas R., *Le Ton beau de marot: In Praise of the Music of Language*, Basic Books, New York, 1997

Homer, *The Odyssey*, trans. Walter Shewring, Oxford University Press, Oxford, 1980

Hornblower, Simon and Spawforth, Antony (eds), *The Oxford Classical Dictionary*, Oxford University Press, Oxford, 1996

Hughes, Robert, *The Art of Australia*, Penguin, Melbourne, 1966

Huysmans, Joris-Karl, *Against Nature*, trans. Robert Baldick, Penguin, London, 1959

Jaffé, Michael, *The Devonshire Collection of Italian Drawings* (4 vols), Phaidon Press, London, 1994

Joske, Prue, *Debonair Jack: A Biography of Sir John Longstaff*, Claremont, Melbourne, 1994

Kerr, Joan (ed), *The Dictionary of Australian Artists: Painters, Sketchers, Photographers and Engravers to 1870*, Oxford University Press, Melbourne, 1992

Klarsfeld, Serge, *French Children of the Holocaust: A Memorial*, trans. Glorianne Depondt, New York University Press, New York, 1996

Koval, Ramona, *Too Many Walnuts: Jewish Cooking, Jewish Cooks*, William
    Heinemann, Melbourne, 1993

Kurlansky, Mark, *Cod: A Biography of the Fish That Changed the World*, Jonathon
    Cape, London, 1997

Lanoux, Armand, *Les Images d'epinal*, Grasset, Paris, 1969

Lawlor, Adrian, *Arquebus*, Ruskin Press, Melbourne, 1937

Leduc, Violette, *l'Affamée*, Gallimard, Paris, 1948

Levey, Santina M., *Lace: A History*, W.S. Maney and Son, Leeds, 1983

Lévi-Strauss, Claude, *Look, Listen, Read*, trans. Brian C. J. Singer, Basic Books,
    New York, 1997

Liddell Hart, B.H., *The German Generals Talk*, William Morrow,
    New York, 1948

Maeterlinck, Maurice, *The Life of the Bee*, trans. Alfred Sutro, G. Allen,
    London, 1901

Mâle, Emile, *Religious Art in France, the Twelfth Century: A Study of the Origins of
    Medieval Iconography*, Princeton University Press, Princeton, 1978

Malraux, André, *Le Monde chretien*, Gallimard, Paris, 1944

Melville, Robert, *Erotic Art of the West*, Weidenfeld & Nicolson, London, 1973

Michelet, Jules, *Histoire de France*, Marpon and Flammarion, Paris, 1884

——*Histoire de la revolution française*, Gallimard, Paris, 1952

Murger, Henri, *Scènes de la vie de bohème*, Hamish Hamilton, London, 1949

Nicholl, Charles, *Somebody Else: Arthur Rimbaud in Africa 1880–91*, Jonathan
    Cape, London, 1997

Ovid, *Metamorphoses*, trans. A. D. Melville, Oxford University Press, Oxford, 1986

Parinaud, André, *Les Peintres et leur école Barbizon: Les origines de
    l'Impressionisme*, Bonfini Press, 1994

Pellaprat, Henri-Paul, *L'Art culinaire moderne: La bonne table française et
    étrangère*, Comptoir Français du Livre, Paris, 1936

Perry, Peter and Perry, John, *Max Meldrum and Associates: Their Art, Lives and
    Influences*, Castlemaine Gallery and Historical Museum, Castlemaine, 1996

Pope, Alexander, *Collected Poems*, J.M. Dent, London, 1924

Quignard, Pascal, *Le Sexe et l'effroi*, Gallimard, Paris, 1994

Rawson, Philip, *Erotic Art of the East: The Sexual Theme in Oriental Painting and Sculpture*, Weidenfeld & Nicolson, London, 1973

Rimbaud, Arthur, *Correspondance, 1888–1891*, Gallimard, Paris, 1965

Ripa, Cesare, *Baroque and Rococo Pictorial Imagery 1758–60*, Dover, New York, 1971

Roettgen, Steffi, *Italian Frescoes: The Flowering of the Renaissance, 1470–1510*, trans. Russell Stockman, Abbeville Press, New York, 1996

Rolland, Romain, *Jean Christophe*, A. Michel, Paris, 1931

Ross, Barbara, *The Chef's Table: An Australian Gourmet in the Great Restaurants of France*, Allen & Unwin, Sydney, 1990

Sand, George, *Histoire de ma vie*, Calmann-Levy, Paris, 1880

Sartre, Jean-Paul, *No Exit: A Play in One Act*, adapted from the French by Paul Bowles, French, New York, 1958

——*The Flies*, trans. Stuart Gilbert, Hamish Hamilton, London, 1965

Schlumberger, Gustave, *Le Siège la prise et le sac de Constantinople par les Turcs en 1453*, Plon-Nourrit, Paris, 1922

Sheridan, Alan, *André Gide: A Life in the Present*, Hamish Hamilton, London, 1998

Souchal, François, *French Sculptors of the 17th and 18th Centuries: The Reign of Louis XIV*, Cassirer, London, 1977

Steinbeck, John, *The Grapes of Wrath*, Heinemann, London, 1939

Stendhal, *De l'Amour*, Gallimard, Paris, 1980

Supervielle, Jules, *Oublieuse mémoire*, Gallimard, Paris, 1949

Vovelle, Michel, *La Mort et l'occident de 1300 à nos jours*, Gallimard, 1983

Waller, Charles, *Magical Nights at the Theatre: A Chronicle*, Gerald Taylor Productions, Melbourne, 1980

Whitaker, Robert, *The Unseen Beatles*, Collins, San Francisco, 1991

Woledge, Brian; Brereton, Geoffrey and Hartley, Anthony (eds), *The Penguin Book of French Verse*, Penguin, London, 1957

Zeri, Federico, *Behind the Image: The Art of Reading Paintings*, trans. Nina Rootes, Heinemann, London, 1990

Zweig, Stefan, *Amok*, Viking Press, New York, 1931

——*Beware of Pity*, trans. Phyllis and Trevor Blewitt, Cassell, London, 1948

PHOTOGRaPH SouRCes

While every effort has been made to locate the copyright holders of photographs, the publisher welcomes hearing from anyone with further details.

FIRST INSERT

PAGE 3 all photographs by Paulette Leguézennec

PAGE 6 (bottom left) Georges Mora

PAGE 7 Georges Mora

PAGES 11–12 Gordon de l'Ile

PAGE 14 (bottom right) Harry Youlden

PAGE 16 both photographs by Brian McArdle

SECOND INSERT

PAGE 1 (top) Mirka Mora; (bottom) Brian McArdle

PAGE 2 (top) Gordon de l'Ile; (bottom left) Georges Mora; (bottom right)
Gerard Vandenburg

PAGE 4 (top) Mirka Mora

PAGE 5 (top) Albert Tucker; (bottom) Harry Youlden

PAGE 6 (top left and bottom left) Harry Youlden

PAGE 8 (bottom) Mirka Mora

PHOTOGRAPH SOURCES

PAGE 9   (top) Geoffrey Smith; (bottom) Robert Whitaker

PAGE 10   (top) Martin Sharp

PAGE 12   (top) Rennie Ellis

PAGE 13   (top) Mirka Mora; (bottom) Henry Talbot

PAGE 14   (bottom right) Serge Thomann

PAGES 15–16   all photographs by Serge Thomann

iNDEX OF PEOPLE aND PLaces